Postcards
from the
Other
Side

Michelle and Ezio De Angelis

Postcards
from the
Other
Side

inspired
LIVING

ALLEN&UNWIN

Authors' note: Names have been changed to protect privacy.

First published in 2012

Inspired Living, an imprint of
Allen & Unwin
Sydney, Melbourne, Auckland, London

83 Alexander Street
Crows Nest NSW 2065
Australia
Phone: (61 2) 8425 0100
Fax: (61 2) 9906 2218
Email: info@allenandunwin.com
Web: www.allenandunwin.com

Cataloguing-in-Publication details are available
from the National Library of Australia
www.trove.nla.gov.au

ISBN 978 1 74237 996 8

Set in 12/18 pt Apollo MT by Post Pre-press Group, Australia
Printed and bound in Australia by Griffin Press

12

Contents

This book is dedicated with sincere thanks to the three couples who have generously allowed us to share the stories of their children—Christine and Todd, Don and Marion, Kerry and Paul—and to all who have loved and lost and will one day be reunited.

We also wish to express our profound gratitude to Maggie Hamilton for her belief in us and our work and to the great team at Allen & Unwin. Thank you all.

For all of you who have supported our work over the years in so many ways, such as by attending our shows, courses and private readings, we hope you enjoy the book and are inspired by the stories in it. You know your loved ones are never more than a thought away.

And finally to our spirit guides—Red Eagle, Sarah and all those who work with us as part of our spirit teams—our appreciation is boundless. Our work and the comfort and healing it brings to so very many would be impossible without you.

Introduction

The life of a professional medium is by turns exhilarating, exhausting, joyful and profound. It is also very, very rewarding.

We can be a hit at social functions or a scary curiosity to be avoided at all costs lest we use our psychic abilities to 'read' a person and reveal their deep dark secrets to the world. Just for the record, this we would never do!

On various occasions we have had the privilege of being shown, even of feeling firsthand, the precious moments of death—when a soul makes the transition from this world into the next. This is an intensely personal event in the journey of any soul. We have even experienced the wonder of communicating with the spirits of babies who are yet to be born to their joyously expectant mothers.

Primarily we act as messengers for the spirit world—reuniting those who have departed this life with their loved ones who remain on earth. We listen, we talk, we counsel, we write, but most of all we learn.

And for as much as we learn, there is always more to know. Our neighbour Michael brought this home yet again just recently, raising a subject as old as time.

'I see that you're doing a show at our local club in November,' he said, before gesturing towards his wife watering the garden in their front yard. 'Some friends of ours saw the banners on display at the club and bought tickets. We thought we might come along too.'

'Great,' Ezio replied. 'Hopefully you'll enjoy it. And you never know, maybe one of your relatives will come through and say hello.'

'Oh, I don't know about that,' Michael said, chuckling ruefully. 'I'm a bit of a fence-sitter when it comes to that sort of stuff. Hope that doesn't offend you.'

'God, no,' Ezio assured him. 'Each to their own. I'm used to people having all sorts of opinions and theories about the work we do. No, I'm not offended in the least.'

'It's not that I don't believe in *anything*,' Michael continued. 'I'm just not sure what I *do* believe in. I mean, regardless of what anyone thinks about life, something had to start it all, right? I mean, at the very beginning . . . before the big bang . . . who lit the fuse?'

Before the big bang?

Good question. And certainly one we have pondered ourselves.

Introduction

Realistically, it is a question we might never be able to answer because, regardless of the discoveries we make about the origins of life, we will always be plagued by the dilemma of what came *before that*.

So why not work on answering the questions that we *are* able to answer?

The evidence for life is literally right in front of us. The problem with trying to understand the world purely through quantifiable physical observation is that you will inevitably miss the power that breathes life force into living things. That power is spirit. You can't measure spirit but you can certainly witness its impact as well as its absence.

To gain a better understanding of physical life we need to first realise that existence of any kind is not possible without the presence of a spiritual life force. Without it, the human body stops functioning. As mediums we are able to communicate with the spirits of those who have left their bodies behind, which can mean only one thing: Life force is contained within the spirit . . . not the body.

If you want to examine some of life and death's bigger questions, who better to ask than someone who has actually lived, died and lives again in the spirit world? A lot might be learned from someone who has survived such a journey. And while they may not be able to provide answers to all of the really big questions, at the very least they might share a little inside knowledge. This is what we have done in *Postcards from the Other Side*. We have asked the spirits of ordinary people to tell their stories. After all, they are a step closer to the *real* action than the rest of us.

One of our favourite sayings is 'Spirits are people too,' because it acknowledges that even though someone may have left their body behind, they are still fundamentally the same person they were before they died. But knowing that people will always see the world from their own perspective, we need to consider a variety of stories. One spirit—being only one person—may not be able to answer all our questions, but add the answers together and you begin to create a picture of what is really important. Each one shares their own unique and special insight.

The insights and stories of these individuals combine to provide us with important pieces of the jigsaw that we call life—and how wonderful to be able to access these pieces of the puzzle while we are still here!

PART ONE

Planning the Journey

1
Dead at sixteen—
T.J.'s story begins

'The newspapers said it was about graffiti,' Christine told us in disbelief. 'It was never about graffiti. It was about loyalty. Toddy was the most loyal person you could ever hope to meet. In the end it got him killed.

'When that knife went through his heart . . . well, it killed me too. Killed my whole family. I don't know how we can ever recover.'

'I don't think you can,' Michelle replied honestly. 'But somehow, with the love and support of your friends and family, you will eventually find a way to live with it.'

Christine didn't believe her.

T.J. was almost seventeen years old when he was stabbed through the heart and died on a suburban street last year, just minutes away from his family home. His parents, Christine and

Todd Senior, were woken late that night by a police officer asking them to come to the local hospital. Their youngest child, Todd Junior or T.J. as he was known, had been injured during a fight and they needed to get there quickly.

'I kept on asking them, begging them, to tell me what had happened but they wouldn't say. All they said was, "You need to be at the hospital." No one would tell us that he was okay. Deep down we knew it was bad but you just hope . . .' she said wistfully, her words and thoughts drifting into a world of what might have been.

'A mother knows,' she said, fighting back tears. 'I could feel he wasn't with us anymore. What really gets me is that the papers made it out to be a fight over tagging.'

'Tagging?'

Christine explained that apparently a kid that T.J. knew— she referred to him as Jason but that isn't his real name—had tagged (written) his street name over another kid's tag. 'That's a big no-no,' she said. 'For whatever reason, it's a big deal to these kids so a bunch of them decided to gang up and bash Jason while he was at a small party at a girl's house. T.J. wasn't even there, but Jason rang him and said that he was in trouble. Apparently, he told T.J. that these guys, some of whom T.J. knew, were threatening to kill him and were going to bash the girl too.

'So T.J. being T.J. ran over there to defend his friend and protect the girl. That's what he was like. Always ready to step up for someone else—even if they didn't deserve it . . . and make no mistake, Jason didn't deserve it.

'Well, a fight broke out and my boy was in the thick of it.

God, he didn't even realise that he had been stabbed, he just kept on trying to protect his friend until eventually he lost so much blood that he fell over. There were five of them. The bastards that killed him just ran away and left him dying on the road.'

No longer able to hold back her tears, Christine looked up and said grimly, 'I will never forgive them . . . I just can't.'

As she told us her story, Christine curled herself into a ball on the settee, her knees pulled up to her chest. Outside, it was as if the world hadn't noticed that T.J. had gone. The sun shone, birds chirped, children laughed and played in neighbouring yards. Life went on as usual. All that stopped at Christine's front door where she had turned the darkened lounge room of her family home into a candlelit shrine for her only son.

2
The itinerary—
Preparing for birth

'There is nothing in the physical world that is permanent,' Shondra, a wise-woman and native elder, once told us. 'And there is nothing in the spirit world that is *impermanent*. Everything you see around you will one day return to spirit. The plants and trees, the birds, animals and people—*Spirit is where we come from . . . Spirit is our home.*'

By any account, this is an elegant summary of the intimate relationship between the physical and non-physical worlds. It teaches us that life isn't only about the things we can see, hear and touch. There's a vast unseen world of spirit as well. This is the life force that drives the physical world.

Although her counsel was greatly appreciated, Shondra didn't tell us anything we didn't already know. As mediums we communicate every day with real people in the spirit realms who wish to convey to their loved ones that they have survived the journey, through the illusion that death is the end, and now live in the afterlife.

How do they do this? By giving us information that proves they continue to exist.

Shondra knows that sooner or later all the things we have in our everyday world will fade away, taking with them everything that we have struggled to achieve during our temporary stay on this planet. She also observes that when everything does fade away, it inevitably returns to the place where it came from. That place is the heart of all creation. That place is the spirit world. And each one of us has an inbuilt GPS (global positioning system) that takes us there even if somewhere along the way we appear to have forgotten the address.

The greatest misconception in the world today is that we are not spiritually connected to the rest of creation through the web of life. We are. Life of every species begins as a soul made from pure spiritual energy in the unseen realms before manifesting into the physical world, and our journey here is never random or without purpose. Our stay on earth might be compared to an extended working holiday in a foreign country where we immerse ourselves in the local culture, attractions, religion and food to gain valuable life lessons and broaden our personal world view.

The knowledge, different experiences and insights such a trip gives you will naturally make you a more complete person. It will impact who you are—mind, body and spirit—with positive flow-on effects resonating through other aspects of your life. This is the goal of our earthly sojourn: to learn and, as a result, to make our spirits more complete. Then, in due course, when we return home to the spirit world, we share our life lessons with other members of our soul family so that they too may benefit from everything we've learned during our journey and similarly we might benefit from their experiences.

The itinerary for our excursion to earth is set well before each of us is born. Some people choose to incarnate together or in such a way as to ensure that their paths cross at some stage during their individual experiences. We have experienced this personally.

In the years before we met, our paths almost crossed many times. We knew the same people and shared many common interests but never actually met until the time was right for us to be together as husband and wife. When that moment finally arrived, there was no stopping us. We were not falling in love for the first time. Our relationship started long ago in spirit. Through psychic visions—and with a little help from our spirit guides—we know that we have spent many lifetimes together. In our previous lives, no matter which part of the world we found ourselves in, or what era, we always seemed to gravitate towards one another and pick up where we left off. Our meeting and subsequent romance is written in our souls' itineraries. We are eternal husband and wife. Ezio's spirit guide, Red Eagle, jokes that we are 'an unstoppable cosmological force'! He is right.

But while a great deal of planning goes into our journey, not everything about our lives on earth is set in concrete. As with any good itinerary, there is an inbuilt flexibility that allows for new choices, adventures, misadventures, experiences and mistakes during the journey. This is what allows us to learn and grow, so that upon return to the spirit world we arrive as wiser and more compassionate people who are better able to contribute to the soul needs of both the planet and each other. That is what we are here on earth for—to help one another gain greater insight into the spiritually significant beings we truly are. Each one of us is a small but essential part of a bigger plan, much like a jigsaw puzzle where the individual pieces fit together to form a picture.

Coming to earth for a lifetime is a heavenly contract between us and God. It's for our soul growth. The broad details of our life and what we hope to achieve here are lovingly put together to ensure that we personally possess the mental, spiritual and physical tools to benefit from what may sometimes prove to be a difficult and harsh existence on the earth plane.

The detail of this plan is imbued within our soul. The soul plan is carried by spirit from lifetime to lifetime, incarnation to incarnation. This master plan is sometimes referred to as our spiritual blueprint—or our soul's itinerary, as we have referred to it here—and while we may never know the exact detail of the plan, we intuitively know when what's happening around us is part of the plan and we feel out of sorts when it is not.

No plan succeeds with only one participant doing all the work, so our personal blueprint is blended with the lives of others we come to earth to reconnect with. Many of the people we interact with at home, at work and in our community were known to us before we were born. That's because they are part of our soul group or spiritual family. Some soul group members choose to travel to earth together so they can be part of each other's life experience. This may go some way to explaining the phenomenon of deja vu—the experience of doing something for the first time while having a powerful sense that you've done it before, or that curious sensation of meeting someone for the first time yet feeling you have known them forever. They are part of your soul plan, helping you to fulfil what you came here to do or learn by making life easier or harder for you through their participation. Prompted by unfolding current events, your soul recollects tidbits of your blueprint and some details are leaked to your conscious mind as memories lost in time. These experiences feel real because they *are* real . . . even when they haven't happened yet.

Many years ago a woman named Margaret described this very experience: 'I was working for a travel company and had to visit an interstate office to try and sort out some difficulties they were having with a ticketing system. As soon as I stepped out of the lift and into the office, I was overwhelmed by a sense of having been there before, even though I hadn't. Without ever having been to that office, I knew that the tea room was located just around the corner and that the state manager's office was the third door down the hallway. *I just knew it!*

'I was completely detached from the experience, sort of floating through it but still so very much a part of it . . . it was strange. Moments before reaching the state manager's office, a thought entered my head—"You are about to meet your husband." We were married two years later!'

This sensation occurred because Margaret had temporarily experienced time differently and briefly glimpsed part of her soul's itinerary as it unfolded before her very eyes. She was able to simultaneously live in the present while stepping purposefully into her own future seconds before it happened. Meeting the state manager who would eventually become her husband was not a random event, it was a scheduled stop on her itinerary. They undoubtedly knew each other in the spirit world. Their meeting was mapped out in the life plan they had mutually devised before being born.

Just why such things are sometimes unexpectedly revealed to people remains a matter of conjecture, but one possible answer might be that the universe doesn't want them to miss what is a very important milestone in their own grand scheme of things. Our spirit guides call this a 'marker in the shifting sands of time'. It is a signpost to show you that you are on track, the spiritual equivalent of scanning a directory board in the local shopping mall and seeing a great big red arrow pointing to the exact spot where you are standing and a sign saying, *You are here!* Knowing where you are on your soul's itinerary can help you map out where you are headed.

In Margaret's case, she was on track to meet the man she would marry and create a family with. Who knows, she and her husband may well produce a child worthy of a Nobel Peace Prize or who discovers a cure for a disease. Or maybe they have created a loving, peaceful union between soul mates, inspiring others with their devotion and commitment to one another. The possibilities are endless.

We can only wonder at what our wise friend Shondra would make of it all. Perhaps she would wink and say, 'It's lucky she didn't lose her itinerary!'

3
Earth bound!

Before we are born we make our plans and draft our itinerary. Then what? Well, it's pretty simple really. We incarnate, or are born, at a time and place that will enable us to experience the people and events that are part of our soul growth this time around.

Although our spirits connect very intentionally and in a planned and purposeful way with our developing physical bodies during pregnancy, they are by no means bound to them for the duration of our time in utero. While a baby is developing in its mother's womb, the spirit of that baby is still free to come and go from its original home in the spirit world. Literally, it has a foot in each world until such time as it must fully commit to life in the physical world. So its spirit floats in and out of its mother's body, making final preparations for a new life on earth.

Being able to communicate with those in the spirit world, we are fortunate enough to have experienced many surprising and delightful examples which prove that our spirits are not tied to our physical bodies. On one occasion during a public reading, a spirit named Mary came through to connect with her granddaughter Grace who was seated at the back of the auditorium. This loving grandmother was able to clearly identify herself and had given several relevant pieces of information which proved without doubt that she was Grace's grandmother when suddenly she changed the subject. Mary mentioned the name of another granddaughter, Jenny, who though not present that evening was Grace's sister.

'Tell Jenny I have the baby here. I've been keeping an eye on him,' she said. An audible sympathetic sigh floated through the room as everyone immediately assumed that Jenny had lost a baby who was now in spirit with her grandmother Mary. But the best was yet to come. Mary continued, 'He is absolutely beautiful and she will be thrilled with him when he arrives!' There was a collective gasp from the audience but no one was more surprised than Grace. She excitedly confirmed that her sister was indeed pregnant and due to have a baby within the next week or two and that she was expecting a boy. You can imagine our delight when six weeks later Jenny arrived at another of our public readings to proudly show us her new little boy, the very one Mary had spoken of!

This wonderful story teaches us that people who have died and left the physical world are able to know and interact with new members of their own family even before they are born, just like Mary did with her granddaughter's baby.

There appears to be no fracture in the timelines of life preventing people of different eras from connecting in the spirit realms—a strong indicator that the afterlife and the Earthbound pre-life are in fact the same place. That place is, of course, the spirit world!

Another instance occurred during a private reading when the spirit of an unborn child made himself known in no uncertain terms. His future aunt, Renee, was astonished when her spirit nephew showed up. This tenacious little one saw an opportunity to influence his own future and was not about to let it pass him by.

'Tell her Callum is *yuck*!' he said emphatically.

Renee was stunned. 'My sister is pregnant,' she said. 'She knows she is having a boy and is tossing up between two names, Callum and Cameron.'

Both of these babies were able to communicate from the spirit world even though their tiny bodies were already here in the physical world—growing inside their mothers. This illustrates perfectly that spirit is not tied to the physical body but exists independently of it. Not only that, it is also further evidence that on our way to earth we have a sense of what's going on and what lies ahead. In both cases the spirits of the babies made appearances during readings with people who would soon become part of their family. These babies knew about their future family connections before they got here. How wonderfully clever of them! While their physical bodies were busy growing, their spirits were equally busy laying the groundwork for their earthly arrival.

At the moment of conception, all that pre-planning for the

soul to make its way back to earth becomes reality as the spirit enters the little collection of cells that are his or her starting point. That is when life truly begins; when the spirit joins the physical cells that will eventually become its new body.

It is not surprising that we don't remember the details of our growth in utero or even our birth. On a spiritual level it is not necessary—our spirits are not anchored, they are still free to roam, and as with any journey there are many last minute details to attend to before the big trip. There are goodbyes to our spirit families—those with whom we share our spirit lives—and final checks to ensure we are as prepared as we can be for the adventure ahead.

In baby Cameron's case that meant making sure he got the name he wanted! While our personal itinerary for life on earth is flexible enough to allow for spontaneous experiences, Cameron's story is further evidence of our soul's inbuilt GPS with all the important destinations preset. Because the identity of his future family was listed on his soul's itinerary, his spirit knew who to contact and where to find them.

Our physical entry into this world is akin to embarking on an extended trip. The process of actually getting here is not remembered because it doesn't need to be. Those memories belong in the realm between worlds. Fresh memories of past lives or recent interactions in the spirit world would only cause us confusion if they were allowed to infiltrate our consciousness in the physical world. And while we bring with us the deeper spiritual lessons of all we have previously experienced, the life we are about to live is filled with enough challenges of its own without being weighed down by the excess spiritual baggage of the past. Best to pack our soul lightly and allow it to be filled with the wonder and experience of this new journey on earth.

Viewed from the relative comfort and timelessness of the spirit world, a lifetime on earth with its inherent problems and opportunities seems easy. When we're in spirit we see physical life as just a short time away from home, with some meaningful reunions with members of our soul group, before we return to the spirit world. At this stage we think it won't be too long before we are home. But once we're here, it can feel like a very different story.

4
Life—Take three deep breaths

As mediums we meet people from all walks of life—the rich and the poor, the lucky and the unlucky, the happy and the unhappy, those who have experienced great tragedy and those who have relatively uneventful lives.

Whatever our life circumstance the important thing to remember is that even though it may be unclear right now, we are here for a reason and we all have roles to play. Many people with a religious or spiritualist leaning will nod sagely and tell anyone who cares to listen that life is just one long test. When you describe life like that, it seems a bit harsh. There are many trials during life, but it's also important to remember there is also great joy, wonder and awe to be experienced if we are open to it. At the same time it's important not to become so caught up with life here that we forget we're not just flesh and blood. As our friends in the spirit world attest, physical life is not all there is. We are souls on an adventure.

Imagine life as a school. There are subjects which are tedious and difficult, but there are also subjects which are fascinating and compelling. There are breaks for recess and lunch where we can simply play or socialise. Yes, there are tests—but not before we've gained enough knowledge to take them. Pass or fail, we will undoubtedly make mistakes and though it may seem like it at the time, it is not, ultimately, the end of the world. We learn from our mistakes and move on.

It does appear, however, that life is just easier for some people than others. The operative word here of course is 'appear'. One person can never really know what another has experienced. If we compare our lives to those of others, we will always find people we judge as better or worse off than ourselves. But in the end there is only one person you can be responsible for and that is yourself.

Incredibly, we have found it is often those who have the most cause to be angry or bitter at their life circumstance who are not. During our work in connecting people with loved ones who have passed over, we have met people who have experienced terrible tragedy yet manage to continue their lives without blaming the world for their misfortune. These people are surely ambassadors for us all—they have chosen difficult itineraries and live their lives in such a way that they inspire others. Ironically, sometimes the greatest tragedy can open the heart just as much as the most profound joy.

Joel is a perfect example of this. We did not meet him during his short time in the physical world but were privileged to meet him as a spirit. Joel's mother, Kerry, had written to a magazine that we work for hoping to make contact with her son through a medium. Kerry's reading was assigned to Michelle who recalls the following.

•

Kerry had been to see a few celebrity mediums in large public shows but each time she left feeling disappointed that Joel had not made contact. Our magazine readings are conducted over the phone and when I began the session the first thing Joel said was, 'Tell Mum to get some tissues and a glass of water.' An interesting start, and one which provided immediate insight into the caring nature of this young man.

As the reading progressed Joel revealed himself to be a truly special person. Though he conveyed a few brief symptoms relating to his illness, he did not reveal the nature of his passing. Joel asked me to mention the frogs to his mother, and she laughingly confirmed that some frogs had recently hopped into the house and invaded her bedroom. It was wonderful evidence that Joel still looked in on his mum from the spirit world. Joel's grandfather then came forward to pass on his love to his daughter and Kerry was delighted to learn that not only had her dad been reunited with his beloved cat, but that Joel's horse was also there with them in the spirit realms.

Joel then spoke about another young man named Jeremy who was now with him in the spirit world. Kerry confirmed that Jeremy had died just over a year ago and had suffered from the same illness. Jeremy lived in America and he and Joel corresponded via email and MSN chat. They had never met face to face but became friends through a support group as a result of their shared adversity, as did their mothers. Jeremy wanted his mother to know that he was not alone and to reassure his family that he was also okay.

Joel went on to talk about his motorbike and a special necklace his mother wears in memory of him. These unique pieces of information were really meaningful to Kerry because they were so personal and specific. Sometimes referred to as survival evidence, these details paint a picture of a person's life that absolutely confirms to loved ones that they live on. Survival evidence is a very important part of a reading—it identifies that the correct spirit is present and still watches over their loved ones. It can be immensely healing and reassuring.

Kerry's reading then took a very unusual turn. Rather than continue with what he could see happening now or sending hellos to those still here on earth, Joel had a far more personal message to convey. 'I am truly sorry, Mum, for the pain my loss caused you but I don't regret that you are my mother. I couldn't have chosen better,' he said. By now the connection I had with Joel in the spirit world was quite clear and his words were flowing. But what he had to say next was even more surprising: 'My life was short but it was important. I affected a lot of people. And I knew I wouldn't be long in your world because I had to go—I have work to do here.'

As mediums it is our job to pass on what we are told by those in spirit. But this was truly worrying. How could I tell a mother whose heart is already broken that her son was okay with dying because he knew he had work to do in the afterlife? Most mothers wouldn't want to hear that. Understandably, they would rather have their child with them. So I explained that this was an unusual occurrence, then I gently relayed Joel's words.

Kerry was not in the least surprised. 'Oh yes,' she said, 'that would be Joel. We often talked about those things. He was interested in philosophy and though only young he studied many things including Buddhism.'

Immediately it became clear to me why Joel had expressed his gratitude at having this remarkable woman as his mother. Even though her broken heart was yet to mend, she was able to set aside her own pain and acknowledge her son's legacy to the world.

Intelligent, handsome and popular, Joel had always been looked up to by his siblings and peers. Then, at the age of fourteen, he began to experience pain and numbness in his body and was eventually diagnosed with multiple sclerosis (MS)—a debilitating disease of the nervous system. Rather than cursing fate as his body deteriorated, Joel handled his illness graciously. Kerry told me that whenever she was feeling overwhelmed by her son's illness, Joel would look calmly at her and say, 'Mum, take three deep breaths.' It was his favourite saying and his way of reassuring her that everything would be alright.

Because of his great love of the ocean, his spiritual outlook and the calm dignity he displayed in the face of his illness, Joel's family and friends dubbed him 'Our Guru of Surfing'. Before Joel passed, his brother Beau made a short film titled

'Our Guru of Surfing', which he placed on YouTube both to honour his brother and to help raise awareness of MS. It is a beautiful tribute and proof of Joel's remarkable spirit.

To say that this reading moved me deeply would be an understatement. I felt privileged to have been allowed to be part of this precious communication between Joel and his mother, both of whom are extraordinary people. Certainly they have been an inspiration to me, and I thank them for it.

When I approached Kerry about including a part of Joel's story in this book, she had no idea what the book was about so we were amazed when in her reply she wrote:

Would Joel ever want it any other way? This is no coincidence, he would have planned this . . . I can't help but have a chuckle, this is so Joel. He loved and loves everyone and was always so forward in spreading that love, but to be in a book??? Oh, he is such a character, he would be just loving all this attention.

But seriously, he was so ill for so many years with his disease, but he was more interested in helping others. He would talk to people on Facebook that he had never met because they needed help. There are so many stories on his Memorial Page from people saying how much he helped them and taught them to have patience and acceptance of themselves and their life, right up to his very last day.

Yes, he was so loved. But of course he was hurt a lot too. But he said that he was here to learn, and when he had learned his lessons it was time for him to go, so he did.

He was no ordinary person, but sometimes I wish he

would have been just an ordinary person and maybe I would have been able to keep him a little longer.

The Saturday following our correspondence Joel's parents were invited to the wedding of one of his friends. Because Joel would have been their best man, the bride and groom decided to release some butterflies during the ceremony in memory of him. Joel's parents were asked to take part in this dedication and each release a butterfly as well. Kerry wrote to us again after the wedding, saying that her butterfly did not seem to want to leave. It landed on her head, then she carried it back to her seat on her hand where it sat for some time before eventually flying away. Coincidence? We don't think so. Spirits often communicate and show signs of their presence through the beauty and innocence of nature.

As for Jeremy, after the reading Kerry contacted his mother Alice and passed on Joel's message, unsure of her beliefs and the reception this information might receive. To Kerry's delight, Alice was very happy to hear from her son and wrote back saying that the knowledge that Jeremy was alright had given her the strength to be able to walk into his bedroom again, and she now talks to him all the time. Even from the spirit world Joel continues to help those who need it in this world!

•

Perhaps Joel had a better handle on his soul's itinerary than most, but that would not have made his journey any easier as his body deteriorated. Nor would knowing that his illness and early death were part of his legacy make his loss any easier for the family and friends who loved him.

There is an old saying that 'God never gives us more than we can handle.' But, ultimately, if we are the architects of our own itineraries, it might be fairer to say that we never give ourselves more than we can handle. Life is a matter of personal responsibility.

While we are here in the physical world, all we can do is strive to be the best we can be. To appreciate life's joys and sorrows and to learn and grow from our experiences and those of others—that is living. We are not meant to know everything right here right now; if we were, we would.

During his short lifetime Joel glimpsed the purpose of his life. He was here to share love. When Kerry understandably cursed his condition and called it 'that damned disease', he would serenely say, 'Mum, it's a gift.'

Perhaps we should give Kerry the last word.

'I have complete faith in Joel,' she wrote. 'I have been learning my lessons and listening now to everything Joel told me that I wasn't prepared to hear before. I wanted to be the mum who could fix everything instead of listening. But Joel would be so proud of me now. I am learning to have patience, to trust in the universe and to "take three deep breaths".'

PART TWO
Unscheduled Transfers and Stopovers

5
T.J. makes contact

'I have never hated or known the evil that lives inside me before now,' Christine posted on Facebook. The social media site had become her outlet—a place where she could share her sorrow, vent her anger, find like-minded souls to empathise with her grief at the loss of her son.

Facebook is many things to many people. For some, it is a way of building cyber friendships. For others, it is way of staying in contact with people they love but don't get to see often. For Christine, Facebook is all these things and more. It is a virtual shrine that she and others can visit at any time of the day or night to honour and reflect upon the life—and death—of her murdered son.

Behind the anonymity of our computer screen, we watched as T.J.'s family and friends waded back and forth through the stages of grief in search of solace, fearing that what initially began as a way of sharing heartache could turn ugly at any moment. Understandably, many of T.J.'s friends felt the need to avenge their 'little brother's' death and spoke openly of reprisals against his attackers. We spoke to Christine about our concerns.

'T.J. was everybody's best friend,' Christine explained. 'I told them to calm down . . . even though every fibre of my being wanted to go out there and kill them too. But I said, "Can you imagine how your families would feel if they lost you like I lost T.J.? If you don't want your own mums to be as devastated as I am, then calm down and let the law take its course." I understand how they feel. There are days when I just want to get revenge too.'

Describing her son's character, she said: 'I don't want to make out that he was a saint. He was cheeky, that's for sure. But he was so loyal and had so much insight for a young kid that you just knew there was something special about him. I think that's why there has been such an outpouring of emo- tion over his stabbing. He was everyone's brother. When he was twelve, he wanted to learn about spiritual matters and did a kids' meditation course for spiritual awareness. None of his friends knew that about him. He wanted to keep it private. But he was also just as likely to go down the road and nick a packet of lollies from the local shop!'

We first learned about T.J.'s murder when we read about it in the Sunday newspaper and we both felt it was a tragic story. What we didn't realise at that time was that Christine had previously been a client of Ezio's and the boy we were reading about was her son.

A few days later, we received an emotional phone call from a young lady named Jerri. 'Hello . . . this is a message for Ezio. My aunty Christine says that you are the only one who can help her. Well, her son, my cousin . . . T.J. . . . was, um, stabbed and killed a few days ago and she needs your help. Can you please call her? She needs you!'

We had to think for a moment. Then it clicked. 'Christine? Oh my God!' Ezio exclaimed. 'Christine the orb lady!'

Many years before this, we had met Christine when she came along to one of our 'Communicating with Spirit' seminars in the hope of receiving some afterlife messages from her mother and brother who had both died a number of years earlier. She showed us numerous photographs of family gatherings that contained spirit images, orbs and misty hazes surrounding the people in the pictures.

While we really wanted to help Christine, it was too soon after T.J.'s death to do a reading. So Ezio rang Jerri and explained: 'A soul needs a little time to settle into the spirit world before they are able to communicate clearly through a medium. We need to give it some time to make sure T.J. is used to his new life. We would be happy to talk with Christine any time she feels like it, if that helps, but we should leave the reading for a bit longer.'

Although it may appear cruel to deprive a grieving mother of connection with her child, we knew from experience that it was the right thing to do. T.J. had left this world abruptly and his spirit would need time to adjust to its new surroundings. On earth, the spiritual life force that entered our body at conception vibrates more slowly than it did in the spirit world. When we die, our life force speeds up again as it leaves our body behind and moves into the lighter, faster vibrations of the unseen world. This is why most people can't see spirits. They are vibrating too quickly to be visible to the naked eye. It's just like a hummingbird. If it sits on a tree branch and flaps its wings, its wings are clearly visible. But when it hovers mid-air above a flower, its wings flap so quickly they are invisible.

Because T.J. was in transition between the two worlds, his spiritual vibration would still be fluctuating between physical and spirit, just like it would have been when he was a baby in the womb, except that T.J. was now headed back to the spirit world. Although this does not prevent us from making a connection, it does not facilitate the *best possible* communication. There is also the issue of his mother's shock. No one expects a mum to stop grieving, but grief and shock cause a cottonwool-like effect on a person's consciousness, which can cloud their ability to think clearly during a reading. This can often be interpreted by the spirit as a sign that their loved ones don't wish to make contact with them, even though nothing could be further from the truth. So all things considered, it was best for Christine to wait a few months to give the session the most chance of success. Gracefully, but with a heavy heart, Christine accepted our advice.

When the day finally arrived for her session, T.J. did not disappoint, vindicating our decision to hold off until he was strong enough to come through clearly. Ezio recounts the reading.

•

As I welcomed Christine and her daughters, Rhiannon, 22, and Teigen, nineteen, into my reading room, T.J. was standing nearby. I breathed a sigh of relief as I had been worried that I might not be able to connect with him. It doesn't happen often in readings, but it does happen—the spirit that someone has come to connect with doesn't show up. As they took their seats, T.J. moved past his mother and sisters and stood just behind my right shoulder, touching my arm to let me know he was ready to go. This simple act had a great calming effect on me as I had been quite nervous about conducting the session. I knew how much making contact meant to them and I didn't want to let them down.

'One was stupid . . . the other was guilty,' T.J. said rather cryptically.

Exactly what he meant by this was not clear so I asked him for clarification. In response, T.J. showed me another young male spirit standing nearby. The young man looked dishevelled and appeared embarrassed to be there. T.J., of course, looked great, as though he had the spirit world at his feet. Some people are just destined to shine.

'He died of a drug overdose not long ago,' he said, gesturing towards his companion. 'It wasn't intentional, it was an accident. He knows it was stupid. Tell them he is alright and that I am looking after him.'

I relayed this information to his mother and sisters.

'Oh my God!' Christine exclaimed incredulously as the three women exchanged glances. 'That's his friend, James! T.J. died in October and James overdosed a month later.' Christine explained that James's friends and family worried that he might have taken his own life. 'We thought it was because he was so upset about what happened to T.J. They were pretty close.' She was relieved to know it was accidental.

The two boys stood side by side, happy to be reunited in the spirit world, even though both felt the enormity of their families' heartache. Then T.J. expanded upon his earlier comment: 'One was stupid . . . the other was guilty. Guilty of a big mouth. If I had shut up, I would still be there.'

The recipe for good mediumship requires the blending of a number of qualities to bring about the best validation that a deceased loved one still lives on. It should also bring about as much healing as possible. So a medium is required to be counsellor, priest, confidante and message bearer. But all that means little unless the medium is also able to prove that they are truly connecting to an intelligent living being in the spirit world. That is the centrepiece of our work—proving life after death. To do this, we must be able to give clear evidence that the spirit is who they say they are. Next, there must be some proof that the spirit still maintains a high degree of active consciousness and knows what is happening in the lives of the ones they left behind. Only in this way can our clients be certain that we are doing what we claim to do.

I was so grateful that T.J. was able to do all this and more. He struck me as a typical teenager with a great deal of bravado. And while his family grieved his senseless passing, I wrestled with a sneaking suspicion that there was more to be revealed about his life and death. I decided to keep this to myself, fearing that making a martyr of their boy would only add to their suffering or, worse still, spark conflict between his angry teenage friends whom he called his 'crew' and the apparently remorseless people that caused his death.

I could tell that T.J. knew it too. It was the look in his eyes. He had only been in the spirit world for a few months but already he knew that his life and death was about something more than had so far been revealed. But what? I sensed that, somehow, we would soon find out.

T.J. provided a great deal of evidence that day, showing that he knew many things about his family and friends. During the session, he reminisced about places and things that he and his sisters had done together and mentioned Teigen's new hairstyle. He talked of his father and how he fretted that his dad wasn't coping very well, digging himself into a deep dark emotional hole. He mentioned songs that had been written for him and how the laces had gone missing from his running shoes when the police handed them back to his parents. Small details, but personal ones that let his family know he is still nearby.

As the session progressed, T.J. was able to communicate more clearly. Relieved at being able to reunite his family, I kept the session going longer than usual. Midway through our sitting, he brought an elderly woman into the room and happily explained that 'she used to live on Stacey Street, in Bankstown.' The woman was Christine's maternal grand-mother. 'She's great and we get on really well,' T.J. said before adding, 'and Uncle Ricky sends his love too. He wants you to know he was there when I crossed over.' Christine had lost two brothers, Colin and Ricky. Ricky died in a car accident in 1988. It comforted her to learn that her son, brothers and grandmother were together in the spirit world.

Eventually, as one would expect, the session turned towards his murder. 'I should have stayed out of it, Mum. It wasn't my fight,' he said quietly. 'I knew a couple of them which is why I thought I could get away with giving a bit of lip. I'm sorry. I know how much this is hurting you. But you need to know that I gave as good as I got—well, almost. They have caught all of them except one . . . Adelaide.'

Adelaide, the capital of South Australia, is some 1400 kilometres from where T.J. was murdered. It is where the police eventually located the last of his attackers. 'Everyone over here has helped the cops find them,' T.J. said, referring to his spirit family's success in whispering clues and leads into the investigating officers' ears. 'That's how we help . . . suggestions.'

I explained this to his mother and sisters: 'Even though they are no longer participants in the day-to-day happenings on this side of life's veil, spirits can and do sometimes influence what happens in the physical world. They do this by getting in someone's ear and repeating the same thing over and over until eventually the person thinks it was their idea in the first place.'

Christine laughed loudly. 'Well, that sounds like the sort of thing my boy would do.' Rhiannon and Teigen laughed through their tears, vigorously agreeing with their mum. If there was any way in which T.J. could help capture all his assailants, his mum and sisters had no doubt he would.

It takes a lot of energy for a loved one in spirit to make themselves known. As the spiritual energy needed to sustain a connection to T.J. waned, the session drew to an end. Soon, T.J. would have to retreat to the heavenly realms of spirit, safe in the arms of those who now loved and cared for him in the world unseen. I waited for them to show up, expecting to see grandparents, relatives, people familiar to T.J. To my surprise—and shock—it was my spirit guide and mentor, Red Eagle, who came to escort T.J. away. Surely my eyes deceived me?

'He is with Red Eagle!' I exclaimed. 'I can't believe it! I have never seen that before.'

Red Eagle and T.J. seemed to know each other. I couldn't be sure if they had only recently met or if they knew each other well before T.J. was born. Either way, they appeared to be a very important stop on each other's spiritual itinerary. Time, I was certain, would reveal more.

'I am envious of T.J.,' I admitted to Christine, overwhelmed by my own emotions. 'There has to be a reason that Red Eagle and T.J. would walk out of my reading room together. You are obviously right. There must be something special about your son otherwise Red Eagle wouldn't be with him.' I really struggled to explain my feelings. 'I can imagine how much you miss him. If I were to lose one of my own kids, I would be shattered and not sure if I could ever recover. But I just can't describe how I feel right now. T.J. is with Red Eagle! I have spent most of my adult life looking forward to meeting Red Eagle again when I eventually die and leave this world, because he has been such a wonderful guide and mentor to me. I'm so jealous. *Your son is with my spirit guide!*'

Christine listened intently, taking it all in. She smiled wanly. 'You don't know how envious I am of your spirit guide,' she said eventually. *'He is with my son.'*

As my mentor and the young man walked away, I knew that we had not seen or heard the last from this unusual pairing. With Red Eagle involved, there were life lessons to be learned—big life lessons. He is, after all, the greatest spiritual teacher I have ever known.

Just before he left T.J. turned and looked directly at his mother. For a split second, I wondered if she could feel the penetrating brightness of his blue eyes as they pierced the veil between worlds. 'I am not angry, Mum,' he said. 'I only wish I could take away your pain. Sorry you have to go through this. I have no hate or anger towards the boys that did this. None.'

As I solemnly conveyed his sentiment and words, Christine broke down and cried. 'He never did have anger or hate in him,' she said. 'But it doesn't matter now. I have enough hate and anger for everyone. I wish I didn't . . . but I can't help it.'

6
Checking out early

Here on earth, we like our lives, and to some degree our inevitable deaths, to proceed in an orderly fashion. But that isn't always how it happens. The death of any loved one brings about a deep sense of loss for those left behind but it seems easier to cope if the loved one had a full and productive life. Our natural sense of order is tested when someone appears to have died before their time. We believe that children should outlive their parents; that the old should die before the young. This is how the cycle of life and death is meant to be. Isn't it?

If there is one thing above all others that the spirit world has taught us, it is that no one actually dies *before* their time. We return to our true home in the spirit world when our time here is done. For some people, that may take 85 years. For others, it may be no more than a few minutes, days or weeks. Even so, grief is still painful.

Elizabeth came for a reading hoping to connect with her mother in spirit. As the session began, she was initially puzzled when the first spirit to communicate began describing a nursery. Spirits often communicate by projecting their thoughts, emotions or images into the medium's mind. In its most simple form, this process might be described as letting the medium see through the spirit's eyes. We see what the spirit sees. These scenes are a form of clairvoyance and are particularly useful to us when the spirit does not speak the same language or had never spoken a word aloud when they were alive. Using this technique, this spirit was able to show us the colour of the room, the furniture and the Disney characters on the walls. All great stuff, but apparently unfamiliar to Elizabeth who was sitting there hoping to hear from her mother.

The spirit was a baby boy and Elizabeth seemed unsure about his place in her world until he explained that although the nursery had been prepared for him, he had never physically made it there. Recognition and shock passed quickly across Elizabeth's face as the baby boy continued, saying he was with all his brothers and sisters who, like himself, had also never been physically born. 'Oh my God!' she exclaimed. 'My sister has had *twelve* miscarriages—this is one of her babies!' As the reading continued Elizabeth's mother eventually joined in, asking her to reassure her sister that the babies were safe and well with their family in the spirit world.

Babies who have been miscarried, terminated, stillborn or survived only a short time after being born regularly come through during readings. The reason for their short physical stay is rarely explained in terms that make sense to grieving parents, but most are able to find some comfort in discovering that, for whatever reason, their little one was not meant for this world. Occasionally, we are shown their tiny bodies were experiencing physical or developmental difficulties in the womb. If a life with such challenges was not part of their destiny then they return to the spirit world—most likely with a view to being born at a more appropriate time in the future.

Not being born is a very personal soul itinerary issue. Truthfully, other than looking at nature's reasons for terminating a life, we don't know a lot about it. What we do know is that they continue to grow in spirit, maintaining a link with their families here on earth. Many babies who have died tell their families during readings that they act as a kind of guardian angel for their brothers and sisters who *were* born, citing a soul family connection they shared in the spirit world before any of them came here. Perhaps these are the most unselfish spirits of all—touching those here on earth briefly yet deeply before returning to assist them from the world of spirit.

Sudden and unexpected death is always the most difficult to deal with. So many people come to see us consumed with regret over words left unsaid, an unresolved argument, or simply because they didn't get a chance to say a proper goodbye.

This was the case with Janet. She came for a reading to connect with her brother Tony, who died at the relatively young age of 32. Though close as children, they had drifted apart as adults. Their relationship had soured because they disagreed on so many social issues and Janet had often voiced her disapproval of Tony's lifestyle choices. When he was killed instantly in a car accident, Janet was distraught. 'We may not have agreed on many things,' she said during the session, 'but I always loved him and I want him to know that. I miss him so much and wish I had been a better sister.'

Tony came through loud and clear during the reading and acknowledged that although their relationship had been rocky he loved Janet and could understand her point of view better now. This was because Tony now had a wider perspective, what we refer to as a spiritual world view. With the clarity that life in the spirit world delivers, he had let go of many of the issues that had seemed so important during his earthly life.

Reuniting people such as Janet and Tony and watching as they set aside petty jealousies, disagreements and resentments has taught us that those in the spirit world rarely hold grudges over matters that seemed so important when they were on earth. In the relative tranquillity of the afterlife where the seeds of life are sown, earth issues appear trivial. Death is a great teacher—both for those of us in this world and for those in the next. Death teaches perspective by cutting to the core of what is important. And what is most important is love. Although love may sometimes be obscured behind life's other challenges, the bonds we develop here in the physical world are strong enough to keep us connected with those who have returned to the world of spirit. Our work as mediums shows clearly that love never dies. It is an observation worth remembering.

Having a say in the planning of our own lives is of great benefit once we return to the spirit world. Dying suddenly will undoubtedly bring a brief period of confusion as we realise that we have in fact crossed over and are now a spirit. It takes a short while to adjust to our surroundings. Family and friends quickly gather, reminding us that we are home, that we belong. Our soul recalls the details of its life and death as another earthly life cycle comes to an end. Our sudden departure was not a mistake. It was a process designed to help our soul grow and expand. Reunited with members of our soul family who had journeyed ahead of us, we remember the big picture. This applies even in the most tragic of cases such as suicide or murder.

There are many psychics and mediums who have ambitions of working with the police on unsolved murders. In our experience, this can only be effective if the murdered person in the spirit world wishes to cooperate. Most times they don't . . . or can't. Once we have died, the life we left behind is no longer our responsibility. Although frustrating for those whose lives have been shattered by the murder of a loved one, it has been our experience that, more often than not, the victim has found some kind of peace with their death.

Rebecca's reading is a perfect illustration of how a murder victim moves on in the spirit realms, even though the family left behind still suffers. Her 23-year-old brother Matthew had died in suspicious circumstances but the police were unable to gather enough evidence for an arrest. Matthew's spirit came forward immediately and began to pass on details, identifying himself as well as the names of family members and friends to whom he wished to send his love. Rebecca acknowledged all that he said but wanted answers—was he actually murdered and if so who was responsible?

Matthew refused to provide them. He held up his hand in a gesture to stop her questions and pleaded with her to just let it be. He assured Rebecca he was well but his main concern was the toll his sudden death had taken on the family—and any possible recriminations against her or their family that might arise as a consequence of her enquiries. Matthew was protecting them. He did not want the lives of those he loved destroyed or endangered. 'I played with fire and got burned,' was the only explanation he would give regarding the manner of his death. He was adamant that they should let it go and try to move on as best they could. 'They should just live their lives. Tell them that . . . and tell them I love them.'

Viewed with the understanding that we have a say in our own life and death, Matthew's stance makes a little more sense than it otherwise would. Our plans are custom-designed so that we may experience and learn what we need to while we are here.

The other important fact we have learned by communicating with spirits who have left the physical world in a sudden or violent way is that they did not feel the physical pain of their deaths. Many have told us this. Because the actual event that brought about their departure was planned, everyone was ready to facilitate a transition between worlds. When the spirit leaves the body at precisely the right instant, physical injuries, even though they may be extensive, are not actually felt. This is because life belongs to the spirit, not the body. The body is just the vehicle that carries the spirit through its time on earth.

It is a blessing that we do not have foreknowledge of our

own deaths. It enables us to live fully without worrying about our impending demise. Certainly there are cases where people seem to have an inkling that their time here is drawing to a close. Joan told us an incredible story about her husband Bert who died suddenly. 'It was as if he *knew* that he was going to die,' Joan said. 'He retired, got all his finances and business arrangements sorted then suggested we go and visit our daughter who lives in New Zealand. We hadn't seen her or our grandchildren for over two years. We had barely set foot back on Australian soil when he died of a sudden heart attack. Until that moment he had been as healthy as a horse—full of life!'

On a soul level, Bert may have known his time here was coming to an end. Perhaps some part of his soul's itinerary was leaking through to his conscious mind, creating an urgency to wrap things up, take care of details and important matters.

Other people have reported a strong sense of knowing that a loved one was somehow not destined to live in this world for long. If we knew the appointed time of our deaths or those of our loved ones, it would change the entire way we view and live our lives.

Unexpected departures from earthly lives teach us a very important twofold lesson. Firstly, appreciate your life and live it fully. Secondly, to the best of your ability, be patient with others and be kind at every opportunity so you are always prepared for a sudden departure.

7

There's no place
like hell

'It was more than a dream,' Katie said, remembering the night when her sister who had died from cancer came to visit while she was asleep. 'I knew Marilyn was coming back to ask my forgiveness but I wouldn't give it to her. My heart was closed. She just stood there looking so sad. Then she exploded into flames and I wondered if my inability to forgive her caused her to burn up . . . sent her soul to hell.'

The hell that Katie feared had engulfed her sister does not exist. There is no fiery pit where Satan plies his evil trade in lost souls. No one is banished for eternity—no matter what crimes they have committed. We understand that this concept may offend some people's sense of justice. In many ways, it offends our sense of justice too. If it is reasonable to expect heavenly reward for living a good life, then surely it is equally reasonable to pay for the hardship and distress we may have brought to the lives of others?

It all comes down to what this lifetime has in store for you. If it is in a person's life plan to die through murder, for example, then it must also be in another person's life plan to be the murderer. Both victim and murderer are part of the same soul group, each one playing a role in the other's destiny.

The idea that really bad people who have committed the worst types of crime should be banished to an eternal hell can be quite an attractive one, especially if you are the victim of such a crime and crave justice or retribution as part of your healing process. But in the context of spirituality where each of us is part of others' life experiences, one needs to consider the big picture and ask what would be achieved by such exile.

Imagine that we are all actors and that planet Earth is the ultimate big stage production. There are heroes and villains, central characters and innocent bystanders. In the theatre of life, we each have an important role to play. Losing even one precious soul to eternal damnation is not only the waste of a good resource, it is like throwing away a small but important piece of the production. You can still put the rest of the stage show together and get an idea of what the storyline is meant to be but it will never be complete. It will never be whole.

Good and bad cannot exist without each other as one actually defines the other, much like night and day define each other. Without the contrast, everything would look and feel the same. These distinctions help shape human experience. For example, some of the worst atrocities that humanity has perpetrated on one another have brought about the biggest changes in attitude. It is difficult to be ambivalent when you are confronted by horror. Tragedy and heartache also bring out compassion and a sense of community spirit.

Hell in the spirit world is not a place. It is a *temporary* state of being where we reside until we take full responsibility for our actions and account for any pain and suffering we may have caused during our lives. Taking personal responsibility for good and bad deeds carried out on earth is essential to each soul's progress in the spirit world. We need to accept accountability for what happened during the life we have just led. This is not always easy.

In the physical world, the line between being the spirit planning our life adventure and the actual person living it becomes blurred. We find it easy to accept positive experiences as a statement of who we are and where we fit in, but do not find negative experiences nearly so easy to accept. However, both are beneficial to and necessary for our soul's growth.

Confronted by the pressures of living in a physical world that does not always lend itself to our highest and best spiritual ideals, we easily lose our way. And what had started out as an exercise in learning more about love and a shared spiritual adventure with members of our own soul family gradually becomes about other things as we struggle to survive on earth. Down here, there is an overwhelming temptation to live life only for ourselves; to convince ourselves that our daily interactions with others don't really mean that much.

In the spirit world, we account for our misdeeds by personally feeling the enormity of the pain and suffering we brought to the lives of others. These sensations are felt more acutely in the spirit world than they are in the physical one. If, for example, someone murders another person during their time on earth, not only would they feel any pain they inflicted upon the victim, they would also feel the sorrow and helplessness of the victim's family and friends. This applies equally to any act of cruelty, not just murder.

This is about as close to hell as any soul will ever get. It is a state of emotional and spiritual reflection which enables us to feel what others have experienced so that we may live more compassionate lives in future incarnations.

The Buddhists believe that hell is a psychological state of mental, spiritual and physical discord. You don't need to be anywhere in particular to experience hell. You carry it around with you through jealousy, guilt and any number of negative emotions or addictions. To this end, hell is just as likely to be found on earth as it is in the spirit world.

Katie was living in her own private hell—a state of discomfort brought about by her inability to forgive her sister when she lay on her death bed. Marilyn had always been jealous of Katie's life, envying her looks, her successful marriage and her beautiful home. Over the years, Marilyn became increasingly hostile and eventually Katie was forced to take out a protective restraining order against her. Being unable to forgive her sister before she died had become an enormous burden to Katie and something had to be done about it. Guilt, anger—and perhaps a touch of curiosity about whether or not life as a spirit had changed Marilyn's attitude—led Katie to our door.

During Katie's sitting, Marilyn was reluctant to say much at first. When told this, Katie simply rolled her eyes. 'Some things never change,' she quipped. Marilyn huffed. She appeared unsurprised by her sister's attitude.

Eventually, Marilyn whispered, caution and trepidation evident in her tone, 'I want to ask her forgiveness. I know it was all my fault. I am sorry for everything I did to hurt her. Please tell her that I am so sorry.'

Towards the end of her life, Marilyn had time to think about her relationship with her sister and tried to make amends. But the pain she had inflicted made it impossible for Katie to forgive her before she died. As a spirit, she was now taking the opportunity to make things right. It was up to Katie to take the next step.

Katie was taken aback and visibly fought to control the tears that welled in her eyes. 'She said that? She said that it was all her fault? I didn't think I would ever hear her say it.' The floodgates opened and Katie began sobbing uncontrollably. She had been given another chance to restore their relationship. After a while she composed herself enough to continue. 'It wasn't all her fault. I was always jealous of her too. She was always the lucky one; the favourite one. When she got sick, I couldn't bring myself to accept her apology. Then she died and it was too late.'

Katie's dream had graphically shown her the importance that forgiveness played in her sister's journey back to the spirit world. Without it, Marilyn was floating in limbo, a state of uncertainty or of being kept waiting for something. She was unwilling to progress in the spirit world until the situation was resolved. From our outsiders' point of view, however, it seemed that Katie was in a more turbulent emotional state than her sister, even though Marilyn was in spirit and she was still here. Had Katie not decided to make contact Marilyn may have chosen to remain in this state until they were reunited in the spirit world and were given the opportunity to forgive each other there.

It is important to realise that 'hell' and limbo are self-inflicted—choices we make through our own thoughts and actions. Although Marilyn was in a kind of limbo it was of her own making. She had chosen to stay close to her sister and wait for just the right moment to seek her sister's forgiveness so she could continue her journey in the afterlife. Now that her apology had been delivered—and more importantly accepted—she felt free to move on and receive the healing available to her in the spirit world. As for Katie, she too had learned from her relationship with her sister. Because of their mutual experience and the relief she now felt, Katie vowed to be more compassionate and understanding in her dealings with other people. It was a lesson that neither soul would forget.

Although it may seem surprising, those in the spirit world often benefit just as much if not more from a reading than their earthly counterpart. The reconnection through bonds of love unsullied by earthly issues allows a freedom of expression that may not have been possible while they were here. Many spirits receive great healing from the opportunity to set things right with those they have left behind. This helps them to move on with their journey back to the spirit world, freeing them from whatever hell or limbo they have inflicted upon themselves.

This is why we say that, as mediums, our service is to those in spirit rather than those who are still living. We are the earthly representatives of our spirit team, building a better relationship between the worlds. We have had the privilege of communicating with the same spirits many times over as their loved ones come to see us year after year, happy that through our mediumship they are able to keep in touch. It is a role we feel humbled and privileged to fulfil.

Although we are message bearers, we are also students of the mystery of life and death. Being able to observe firsthand how a soul thrives and evolves in the spirit world is an honour we always cherish. And while we have received countless emails, notes and words of thanks from people grateful for what we do, learning from those who have lived and died . . . well, that is truly a gift to us.

8

Lost passports and misplaced souls

Lost spirits, earthbound spirits, doomed to walk the earth forever—what does that mean? Basically these are the terms used to refer to those who have died yet supposedly remain 'trapped' here on earth. Now we are delving into the really spooky stuff—the territory of things that go bump in the night. But does this really happen? Can people become 'stuck' between worlds, unable to move into the afterlife?

During one of our talks about mediumship recently, a woman in the audience raised this very question. She had been to see a medium who told her that her son who had died abruptly could not be contacted because he was not yet in the spirit world. He had died almost two years earlier. She wanted to know whether this was true. Given that he was no longer in the physical world, it posed the obvious question.

Where else could he be?

Many times over the years we have counselled distraught parents, children and siblings who have lost loved ones and been told by supposedly experienced mediums that their spirits are trapped between the worlds. In some instances they were told that the family themselves are responsible for holding these spirits back with their grief. Naturally this caused them great distress as they didn't know how *not* to grieve for their departed loved one. Fortunately, nothing could be further from the truth.

Each soul automatically returns to its original source and no amount of grieving will stop its progress. Imagine that you are desperately in love with somebody who has no idea that you even exist. Is the power of your love enough to bind them to you? Of course not. And that is here in the physical world! So how can grief stop a spirit from progressing to where they need to be? The answer is, it cannot. Our emotions are certainly powerful to us but they are not powerful enough to hold back the spirit of another. Another soul's journey is entirely out of our hands.

A more plausible answer for the woman who lost her son might be that, for whatever reason, the medium just couldn't make the connection. This happens occasionally if the medium is not the most appropriate messenger for a particular spirit. Unfortunately, rather than being honest about it, this medium may have chosen to shroud the situation in mystery, dooming the woman's son to be a lost soul instead of admitting that the connection could not be made.

We have, upon occasion, encountered spirits who are not

willing to communicate with their loved ones through a medium. Spirits, like people, have free will and their reasons for not communicating are many and varied. For some, it may be that they retain religious beliefs that forbid spirit communication. Personality and timing play a part as well. Some spirits are shy and reserved while others may just not be ready to make a connection. Others may have difficulty with the process of conveying their thoughts and feelings to a medium.

Communicating through a medium is not something spirits do every day. This is why we recommend that, before having a private reading, potential clients familiarise themselves with our work by attending our public shows of mediumship. Not only does it give them a valuable insight into what to expect from a reading, it also gives their loved ones in the spirit world a first-hand look at what is required to get through as clearly as possible.

The spirit world does not exist somewhere up in the sky above. It is literally all around us because it is not actually separate from the space we occupy. The spirit world overlays the material world in much the same way as a glove fits over a hand. However, we can't see the spirit world the way we see physical things because it vibrates at a higher energetic rate than the visible world.

In developing our mediumship, we have trained ourselves to perceive the faster moving spirit world through psychic meditation. Through repeated practice and dedication, we have learned to increase the space between our day-to-day thoughts and simply receive spiritual impressions rather than go looking for them. Our guides have taught us that because spirit communication is essentially mind-to-mind communication, this practice facilitates a clearer view into their world. It is like slowing down the speed of a hummingbird's wings so you can see every feather in detail. This is what we refer to when we talk about 'spirit energy' and 'raising our vibration' so that we can connect with those in the spirit world.

When they first lose a loved one, many people are able to feel or sense their presence. Some have sensed a tingling sensation or smelled familiar perfume, while others glimpse shadows and light out of the corner of their eye. There are even accounts where spouses claim to have felt their partner come back and lie on the bed beside them! As time passes, however, the person who has died becomes more attuned to the spirit world and less to the physical one. This makes it more difficult for the spirit to make its presence clearly known to people who are not mediums. Tangible evidence of them still being with us becomes harder for them to generate and gradually fades away as they move further and further away from being a physical person. This can be very upsetting because it feels like losing that loved one all over again. Some clients have said they felt abandoned and asked where their loved one had gone. They haven't actually gone anywhere, they are just as close but are lighter in their energy vibration and find it more difficult to impact the physical world.

This is why mediums exist. We specialise in making connections with those in the spirit world who are unable to let their loved ones on earth know they are still nearby.

Naturally there are exceptions and Ezio's maternal grandmother is one. Ezio's mother Anna keeps a photo of her mother Maria tucked between the glass and timber frame of her dressing table mirror. Although she has been in the spirit world for around 40 years, Maria still makes her presence known. On several occasions when Anna was feeling troubled or in need of comfort, the photo somehow dislodged from the mirror frame and fluttered across the room, landing in some unlikely place on the floor. Quite often, the photo floated sideways a few metres and landed by Anna's feet. There were no open windows or doors to create a draught that might explain the phenomenon.

Because there are few spirits strong enough to generate physical energy like Anna's mother Maria, people here often worry that their loved ones are lost in the spirit world. Generally this is not the case. In the afterlife there is always someone to point the way. If you were on a trip and lost your passport you would go to the appropriate authority or embassy, and there would be people there to help you. So it is with the spirit world—there are always others there to help you readjust to life without a physical body. Loved ones who have made the journey before you will be there waiting with open arms. But, if for some reason, you decided to throw away your passport because you didn't want to return or be found, you would not seek help. Who we meet and what we do in the spirit world comes down to personal choice. There are some who may choose not to move forward for their own reasons. Guilt, fear, remorse, addictions, anger—there are lots of reasons why an individual may choose not to move on immediately. Our personalities play a huge part. We are still the same people and there will always be those who don't want to accept help.

We have even met spirits who choose to remain close to their earthly families for a short period after their deaths to make sure that they were coping with their grief and adjusting to life without them. Once these spirits are satisfied that their loved ones are alright, they embark upon their own journey into the afterlife.

The two worlds mirror each other closely. Just as there are social workers here to help people with their life issues, there are counsellors and healers in the spirit world to assist those with issues arising from their death or transition. A sort of debrief takes place. These beings are highly evolved and have infinite love and patience with souls who have recently crossed over but might still have a few issues to resolve. These souls are the ones who may choose to stay close to the earth plane, but they are not trapped between worlds. When they are ready and the time is right, they too will move on with their spiritual journey.

Now, back to those things that go bump in the night. A few years ago we ran a seminar titled 'What Happens When You Die' and were both very surprised when one of the attendees was a lady named Liz who ran a successful ghost tour company not far from where our centre was located. Truthfully, we were a little concerned because we felt that Liz, who was no shrinking violet, might actually be annoyed that our views would be in direct conflict with her business. Although we acknowledge that ghost tours may have a place in helping some people accept the existence of a spirit world, we are not strong supporters of them. We believe that spirit communication is for healing broken hearts and wounded souls. Chasing spectres around cemeteries at night does nothing of the sort.

Ghost tours have always been popular. People love the thrill of scaring themselves, which is why they ride roller-coasters and watch horror movies. However, most of what is sensed or felt in a 'haunted' place is just the leftover energetic imprint of people or events that have taken place there, not an actual spirit that can be contacted or communicated with. Some places such as old psychiatric institutions, prisons or quarantine stations have a strong imprint due to the misery suffered there. The intense emotions of the inmates is imbued into the walls and floors, the very fabric of the building itself, but it is not the spirits of those who once stayed there. It is just their residual energy or psychic footprint.

Most people can pick up this energy imprint psychically. It is exactly the same as walking into the boss's office and knowing without a word being exchanged that he is in a bad mood and today is not the day to ask for a pay rise! Words are not necessary in such situations—you can feel it.

Many people would be familiar with the psychic practice called psychometry. Psychometry is when a psychic reader receives information about someone while holding an object they own, such as a ring or other piece of jewellery. The object is imbued with the life force of the person who owns it and their experiences can be felt by a trained 'sensitive'. The same principles apply to supposedly haunted buildings and places. They also hold the energy of those who once lived there. This energy is often seen as orbs, smoky hazes, mists or even ghostly apparitions in the shape of a person. These images are easily captured on modern digital photographic equipment. Many people think these are actual spirits but they are just energy imprints.

Fortunately, Liz the ghost tour lady agreed with our explanation of this phenomenon. She made a point at the end of the night of telling us how much she had enjoyed the seminar and felt that we had satisfactorily explained what happens on her ghost tours. Unbeknown to us, Liz had just been diagnosed with terminal cancer so her reasons for attending were actually personal rather than business ones. Liz didn't reveal her illness to us at the time, or on the few other occasions when we met her again briefly, so we were surprised when, on the day she passed away about a year later, her husband called us and asked Ezio to speak at her funeral. It was Liz's request that he do so and we were very touched by it.

If we look at the idea of haunted places logically, it seems very simple. If you had the choice of doing what you wanted to and living where you want to for eternity, would you choose to be comfortable and surrounded with beauty? Or would you choose to spend your afterlife hanging around a dark cold cemetery or creepy old hospital? Where would you prefer to think *your* loved ones are—safe and watching over you or spending their time in the spirit world as an attraction for ghost-hunting thrill-seekers?

Of course, there are cases where those in spirit do make their presence felt—or seen! Recently we had a call from a lady named Julie who lived interstate. She was upset because both she and three of her five children had repeatedly seen a 'ghost' in their house. The most upsetting thing about these sightings was that this ghost appeared wearing her sixteen-year-old son's favourite green T-shirt!

We often receive calls or emails asking for advice from people with similar issues. Seeing spirits in the house is actually quite common, particularly for children up to about the age of seven, who are naturally more sensitive to the spirit world, and for people who have mediumistic tendencies. Once we have ruled out several practical factors that may be the cause of the phenomenon, we look to the usual suspects—their own loved ones in the spirit world. It makes sense that an unexpected spirit visitor is most likely a member of the family just checking up on things.

This proved to be the case with Julie. After asking a few questions, it didn't take us long to establish that their visitor was actually a loved one keeping an eye on his earth family. Julie's sixteen-year-old son had a twin brother who was stillborn. Although in the spirit world from an early age, he had chosen to grow and age along with his siblings. For sixteen years he had watched over his family and gotten to know them. Now it was time for them to know him. Julie was very relieved. She was able to talk to her family about the brother they had never known. Once the spirit teenager had received acknowledgement as part of the family, the disruption from his visits settled down.

No matter what we choose to do with our spiritual passports, with the help of our own personal GPS we will always find the way back to where we belong. We all end up where we are meant to be, even though some people take longer to get there.

Ezio's guide Red Eagle has a name for the many and varied paths that lead us home in the spirit world. With a knowing that comes from his many lifetimes of learning, he smiles and says, 'It is a journey to the light . . . via the long way around.'

PART THREE

Arrival in the Afterlife

9

T.J. describes his death

The image of T.J. side by side with Red Eagle at the end of Christine's reading left a lasting impression.

In all the years that Red Eagle has been Ezio's spirit guide, it was the first time he had openly taken a personal interest in a soul's transition through the spirit world. Our spirit guides do not usually have personal relationships with the people we connect with during our readings. They know that the process of life and death occurs naturally and doesn't need their intervention so they are happy to let things run their course. It is a wisdom—and patience—that comes from lifetimes of learning.

Red Eagle is not the kind of spirit to casually show up at another person's reading. He is a spiritual master and everything he does has great purpose and significance. That is why he is a such a wonderful teacher. Like a river flowing effortlessly to the ocean, he lets nature take its course. He lives and works within life's cycles of ups and downs and teaches us to do the same. But his presence with T.J.? We couldn't help but wonder what message he was trying to send.

Later, Red Eagle explained why he seemed more interested in T.J. than other spirits we had worked with. 'T.J. may have been only young in years,' he said in a measured tone, 'but he has a wisdom beyond those years. A wisdom which goes back many lifetimes. It is sad that his family has lost him in such trying circumstances. No doubt it brings them great pain and suffering. Nevertheless, the young man has agreed to speak of his journey in the spirit world so that you may write of it in a book and share it with others.'

Really? Write about T.J.? In a book? We couldn't see it. Not because we thought T.J. wasn't a worthy subject—far from it. From the incredible outpouring of love and grief following his death, it was obvious that he had touched the lives of many people. But he was only sixteen and we just couldn't see how a boy that young could tell us anything about life that we didn't already know. We shouldn't have been so dismissive. T.J. was right there with the answer.

'I can tell you what it's like to be dead,' he said matter-of-factly.

Then it became obvious to us. T.J. was offering us a chance to draw back the veil between worlds and witness life in the spirit realms firsthand.

His sudden departure was—and still is—tragic. And it certainly devastated those closest to him. Dying young always seems futile, but through his ability to contact us and his family, T.J.'s death seems a little less in vain. His legacy, through living and dying, is that he is able to act as a pioneer in educating those of us still here, perhaps removing a little of the sting of death by bringing the physical world and the afterlife closer together. Not just for himself and his family but for so many others who wonder about what happens to us when we die.

To prove that he was serious, T.J. popped up in the strangest places as if he was trying to confirm his role in bringing this book to life. One time his spirit waltzed into our lounge room and told us that an email from Maggie, our publisher, had arrived on the computer downstairs and that her response to our book proposal was positive. When we checked, the email had in fact arrived just a few minutes earlier. Another time, he entered our reading room during a private session with an unrelated woman and asked that we thank her for the flowers. It turned out that although she didn't personally know T.J. or his family, she worked for a florist and had delivered flowers to his family home as well as his funeral service.

When we told Christine about T.J.'s activities, she wasn't surprised. 'He always loved being the centre of attention,' she said, sighing. 'It's part of what made him the person he was. Last night he came to me in a dream. I was sitting behind the goal posts watching him play rugby league. I was taking pictures of the game when he scored a try. After he scored, he ran over to me and pushed his face right in front of mine. It was the most vivid image of his beautiful face and blue eyes. I could see him so clearly, as if he was only inches away from me. He looked younger than he was when he died. Like he was when he was just a cute loveable kid . . . before he turned into a cheeky teenager. I miss him so much.

'Then the dream changed and the guy that killed him was sitting on the couch in my lounge room. My husband Todd was standing there, yelling at me to get that mongrel out of our house, but the guy just wanted to say that he was sorry. He wanted to let us know how sorry he was for killing T.J. I knew it couldn't bring T.J. back . . . but at least he was sorry for what he did. I guess that's something, isn't it?'

Christine was looking for the silver lining behind the dark clouds that had overshadowed her family's life. She was not yet ready to forgive her son's killer but she now had evidence that T.J. had already done so. Just as she knew he would. 'He could never hate anyone,' she said of her son. 'He was always willing to give people a second chance.'

When she finished telling us about her dream, we sought counsel from Red Eagle. 'The young man is showing his mother the value of remorse and forgiveness,' he said. 'T.J. still considers his mother's house to be his family home. By inviting his assailant into his home—even though it was only through a dream—he is showing her that he is not afraid to forgive those who harmed him. It would seem that the young man has recognised his killer as part of his spiritual family, a member of his soul group. It is a noble and heroic gesture and one that will guide him through his journey in spirit. Forgiveness takes great courage.'

'I don't expect my family to forgive him,' T.J. interjected. 'It's different for me. I am over here and I can see the big picture. They don't see me hanging around listening to music anymore; don't see me in the house or coming home to get changed and then head out. To them, I am gone. But over here you see things differently. It's like seeing things as they are meant to be . . . like it's all part of a plan. I know how much they are hurting and wish I could take it away . . . but I can't do that. I can only try and show them that I'm still alive.'

T.J. then described his death and his journey into the spirit world. 'My family was the first and last thing I thought of on either side of dying. As soon as I crossed over, I knew that they were what mattered most in the life I had just left behind. The people you love are what matters. Mum, Dad, Rhiannon and Teigen were on my mind as I crossed over.

'When I was stabbed, it was like being hot and cold at the same time. My body felt like it couldn't hold on to my spirit anymore and I was being lifted up into the sky, even though I was only a short way off the ground. It felt like I was being pulled away but I wasn't moving. I could see myself lying there and people running around screaming at each other "Call an ambulance!" I wasn't afraid.

'I looked up and the guys who did it were all running away and I thought, "Come back and fight, you gutless bastards!" Then it was like I started shivering—not much, just a little bit—and I felt like I was going to throw up. I don't know what that was, but it felt like I was being pushed or pulled out of my body. I wanted to go back into it but it didn't feel right anymore . . . like I had only just left it and it didn't feel like it was mine to go back to. Weird.

'As I was looking around I could see everything really clearly. I could see the insects on the ground and became really aware of them and how busy they were. I could see birds asleep in the trees and bats flying around in the sky. It was a bit freaky but not scary. Just different. All the noises seemed far away like I was listening to them with my head underwater but I could still make them out even though I wasn't really interested in them. Dying makes you feel like part of the world.

'I saw my body heave a couple of times and each time it did I felt myself being pushed away from it. I know now that it was my spirit moving away but at the time all I could think of was that Mum and Dad were going to be really angry!

'Then I saw Grandma and Uncle Ricky. That's when I knew I wasn't coming back. They had been there the whole time, from the start. As soon as I recognised them, a warm light started shining inside me. That light is still shining inside me and feels good. Uncle Ricky said it never goes out, that it stays with you forever to help you. I think it's God.

'Grandma told me that I was with them now and that we should go to visit Mum and Dad because they were worried about me. I could feel how much she loved Mum. That's the first and only time I felt worried—it was when I realised that I was dead. I knew how much my family loved me and thought that it was going to suck having to lose me. I started to cry because I knew how much Mum had been hurt by people dying before and I thought, "She will never get over this one." We got there just as they were leaving the house. I don't know how long that took. It didn't feel long but I don't know. I could see them running around, looking for stuff, panicking, and Dad was like a zombie on autopilot, just moving but all the time his heart was pounding. *I could hear it!*

'I remember thinking that it was pretty cool that I could look in on Mum and Dad and also keep an eye on what was happening to my body. It was like I was in two places at the same time . . . no, three places . . . it was like I was in heaven with Grandma, at home, and lying there on the street all at the same time. I guess that's what they mean when they say there is no time or place in spirit. It's true.'

T.J.'s description of his death contradicted everything that most people believe about the process of dying. Rather than feeling isolated and frightened, he felt more connected than ever to the world he was leaving. T.J. then described how it felt as he began to settle into the spirit world.

'Then—I'm not really sure when—I started to lose a bit of sight into your world. I couldn't see as much as before. Like when I was stabbed I could be everywhere and see everything. One day I just started seeing only my family and closest friends. It's like the rest of the world didn't belong to me anymore so I couldn't be a part of it. It didn't worry me. It felt natural and okay. I was part of another world . . . a bigger one.

'It felt like I was pure or something. No one actually tells you stuff over here but you sort of just know—or remember, maybe—I don't know, it's hard to describe. It's like every-thing here feels like it's heading somewhere but you don't know where. It just feels right to go with it.

'I started thinking about all the stuff I had done. The good and bad. And I started feeling bad about causing trouble. Then I realised something really strange. Each time I remembered something bad I had done—like stealing or hurting people—I felt really bad about it. But each time that happened, the light inside me would shine really brightly and make me feel better. The light helps you get over the stuff you did that you're not proud of. It was like I was letting go of something. I don't know, letting go of stuff that I had done that was holding me back. And each time I did it, it felt like I was floating down a river on a raft or something, just going with the flow, going somewhere good.

'I don't know how but I knew the cops would catch my attackers. I also felt a bit sorry for them because I knew that sooner or later they would realise what they did and have to fix it up somehow. I know how bad I felt about the small stuff I had done and they had done much worse than any of that. It hurts inside when you realise that you have hurt others.

'Red Eagle told me that over here you find out firsthand that hurting other people really is like hurting yourself. Everyone is part of the same spirit. Apparently, that is why I felt so connected to everything when I died, including the birds and plants and insects. We share the same spirit. I thought I was just seeing them for no particular reason but I was wrong. They were there helping me cross over. We were part of the same world.

'That's why I brought Mum the dream about my murderer being sorry for what he did to me. It's also why I also wanted her to know that I don't hate him for it, even though I admit that I really hate what it has done to my family. I see my life so clearly. Like it's an action movie and I was the star of the show!'

10
Settling into the spirit world

When we are born, our spirit enters our body and we come into being in the physical world. When we die, this process is reversed—we leave our body behind and re-enter the spirit world. What we call death is really more like a new birth into a different place.

There has been lots of research over the years into near-death experiences, or NDEs, which occur when a person 'dies' and then comes back to life, such as when they are resuscitated. Some of the scientific community suggests that near-death experiences are simply the mind playing tricks due to a lack of oxygen to the brain. While this may be phys-iologically true, our guides have indicated that rather than causing mental delusion, the lack of oxygen alters the person's state of consciousness and allows them to witness how the soul enters the afterlife. There is much debate between spir- ituality and science, but the more these two uncomfortable bedfellows work together the more we learn that we are after all a combination of the physical and the spiritual. One of the most revealing results of recent research is that many of those who have had an NDE describe the same experience regard- less of culture, country or religion.

People who have had a near-death experience often describe travelling through a dark tunnel and being drawn towards a very bright light at the end of it. When you think about this, it actually sounds like the way we would describe our entry into this world if we were able to remember it. Out of the darkness of the womb, through the birth canal, into the light. On the way into this life we bring with us a physical body; on the way out of it we leave that body behind. Death is just like the birth process.

Those who have had this glimpse into the next life gener- ally report a feeling of calm and peace and say that they are no longer afraid of dying. These people have an important role in sharing their insights with the world. They are able to tell the rest of us that there is something more 'out there' after physical life ends and that crossing over should not be feared. They literally show us the road to go home and give us hope that human beings do in fact live on after they leave the physical world.

There have also been a few documented cases of near-death experiences where some people have seen less pleasant sights that they struggle to describe in human terms. These images often take on the form of a dark void where nothing seems to exist and the overwhelming feeling is one of loneliness. In the majority of such cases, these people have returned to the physical world with a newfound resolve to live a better life. They feel like they have been given a second chance to get it right so that when they do eventually die they will be able to go somewhere far more pleasant than what they witnessed through their NDE.

Connecting people every day with their loved ones in the spirit world who have gone ahead of them leaves us in no doubt that the spirit does not need a physical body to exist. This observation is supported by NDE accounts where the participants describe leaving their body behind, much as one might discard their clothing. Imagine that you are attending a fancy dress party. You put on a costume which is useful as your identity for the night. At the end of the evening you go home and take that costume off. You are still you and have had the added bonus of the fun and experience that attending the party and wearing that costume brought you. That is what it is like as we move through lifetimes. Our physical bodies are like costumes. When the party is over, we leave behind the costume we no longer need, and are hopefully richer and better for the experience.

Settling into the spirit world is an individual process and each person will handle it differently. Many spirits we have spoken to during readings for their loved ones tell us they were met by a familiar face—a relative, a friend or even a beloved pet who had made the journey into spirit before them. Some spirits even joke that seeing their deceased loved ones in the afterlife made the idea of being dead a much more agreeable one! This is especially comforting for those who died suddenly and without warning. The advantage that arriving in the spirit world has over being born into the physical one is that we arrive with our recent life memories intact. We are very much aware of who we are and where we have just come from. Because of this we have some control over the situation, which helps to remove fear and confusion from what might have been an otherwise challenging experience.

Expectation and beliefs play a big part. Those who are strongly religious may see angels or religious figures; atheists or those who don't believe in the afterlife may initially feel that they are in a void of nothingness; those who have committed atrocities or suffer addictions may choose to stay close to the earth plane for a time (as discussed in Chapter 8). However, these states are a personal choice, and there are those in the spirit world assigned to help each and every soul continue their journey and progress when they are ready.

In cases of suicide, the person who has taken their own life often arrives in the spirit world in a depressed, confused or angry mental state similar to the way they were feeling before they died. Due to religious beliefs, many also fear that they might be severely punished for ending their life prematurely and want to hide from God—whatever that might mean. These souls are often referred to as being trapped or lost, but they are not. They may be temporarily distant from the rest of the spirit world because they choose to be. But they are no more than a change of mind away from being comforted. It is that simple.

Rather than being punished or condemned for their actions, when they are ready to accept the generosity of the spirit world, they receive the healing they need. At some stage they must also face the pain and distress their manner of death has caused to those left behind. This is an essential part of self-healing in the afterlife, but it happens only when each soul is ready so that the process is helpful rather than harmful.

Those who suffered severe illness, physical ailments or disabilities in this world often express a profound sense of relief and say that when they left behind their bodies they also left behind their pain. It is not unusual for us to see them kicking aside their wheelchair or walking frame and demonstrating a few dance steps in an exuberant show of vitality.

Eric was a sprightly and very active man who felt terribly frustrated and restricted by his body in the last years of his life. He had been confined to a wheelchair and needed to use an oxygen tank to breathe comfortably; an automatic action that most of us take for granted. During a reading for his daughter Fran, Eric wanted her to know that he was no longer suffering; that he was healthy and vital again. Returning to the spirit world for Eric and others like him is accompanied by a wonderful sense of freedom. It is often those who had the most difficulty while on earth who find it easiest to embrace their newfound lightness of being and settle into the spirit world.

Like any major change, our personality influences the ease of our spiritual transition. There are always some individuals who are, by nature, more accepting and easygoing than others. Undoubtedly they will take the spirit world in their stride and settle in more easily. Similarly, those who cross over with some degree of acceptance that they are leaving the physical world will come to terms with their new surroundings more quickly. This is obviously not the case for everyone though.

Marcus, a spirit helper of ours who has given us great insight into the spirit world, likes to tell the story of his arrival on the other side. Marcus died young, in his twenties. He was certainly not ready to move on. The circumstances of his death were also very unpleasant, and he is quite open in saying that he was most put out by the entire situation! There he was, young, popular and fabulous, enjoying life and all it had to offer, when all of a sudden it ends abruptly and violently. Furious at this great injustice, Marcus found himself in a whole new place but decided that he was completely uninterested and didn't want to know. Discontented with his new lot in life, Marcus isolated himself and set about having a good sulk. It wasn't long—Marcus admits he was already becoming a bit bored with sulking and being alone—before he was approached by Ezio's main spirit guide, Red Eagle.

For all Marcus's party boy lifestyle and apparently carefree attitude, there was another side to him. Marcus had depth, wit, insight, compassion learned through tough experience and, above all, he was honest to the core. Marcus has told us that he rarely lied to anyone, not even to spare their feelings. It was a sometimes brusque way of living but it was always an honest one. Most importantly, though, he never lied to himself. These are the qualities Red Eagle saw in Marcus when he approached him.

To this day Marcus likes to joke that when Red Eagle asked

him if he would help Ezio deliver messages from the spirit world to loved ones still living, he believed it was a punishment. 'I thought it was because I was gay!' Marcus said with his usual wicked sense of humour. Of course, nothing could be further from the truth.

His story is a great example of the process of settling in— Red Eagle found Marcus when he was ready and helped him find his niche in the spirit world. The qualities that Marcus possesses are perfect for his role as a spirit helper and are precious to us. His honesty and direct approach help us link on a very real level with those in the spirit world and we feel so fortunate that he has taught us so much about life in the spirit realms. And he is a real character and loves being the centre of attention!

Marcus generously sharing his story shows us that arriving in the spirit world and finding your place is a very personal process but not one to be feared. Each of us is part of something bigger—connected to all other living things through the web of life. No matter what your beliefs, religion or state of mind, no matter how you die, we all end up in the spirit world. Each one of us will end up in the right place. If we are lost we will be found. If we are angry we will be granted time to let that anger fade. If we need love and healing we will receive it when we are able to accept it. There are no conditions, no barriers, to receiving all the love that the spirit world has to offer.

Ultimately, we have control over how quickly and how well we settle into the world of spirit when we eventually arrive there. Naturally, like any transition, we have to allow a little time to adapt to new surroundings but being reunited with those we had lost and being freed from the restrictions of the physical body and much of the stress of the physical world undoubtedly aids our progress.

There is an old saying—'When in Rome, do as the Romans do.' This speaks of adapting to your surroundings by blending in with the local culture. It is sound advice within the confines of the physical world because we need to respect the differences between ourselves and others on this planet. We show empathy and respect to others by accepting their customs and ways when we are in their home and generally like them to do the same when they are in ours.

In the spirit world, however, we realise that the divisions and limitations of the physical world are no longer relevant. We don't need to do as the locals do. We are free to truly embrace our surroundings in a manner that suits us. Our souls can truly shine.

11
Religion and culture on the other side

When Lisa was four years old, she asked her father a question: 'Daddy, when you die and go to heaven, will Jesus be there?'

'Yes, he will,' her father replied.

Her father's answer seemed to satisfy her curiosity, but a few minutes later she looked at him earnestly and asked another question: 'Daddy, in heaven, will you see *your* mummy and daddy again?'

This time her father was surprised. He replied, 'Yes, I believe that when I die, I will see my mother and father again, as well as Uncle Mark who died last year.'

Lisa's question about Jesus was a reasonable one. The idea that Jesus would meet Lisa and her family in heaven seemed a natural enough assumption based upon all she had been taught by her Catholic parents. She had undoubtedly heard many good things about Jesus and would have expected to see him in heaven.

But how did the idea arise that her grandparents would meet them there as well? Her parents had never discussed their deaths with her as she was so young. And, because her father's parents died before she was even born, Lisa had never met them . . . or had she?

Maybe Lisa's young soul had been able to tap into some distant memories of her life in spirit, her life before being born into her earthly family. Perhaps her soul remembered a time long ago when she knew her future grandparents?

This is where it gets interesting—how do religion and the spirit world fit together?

There are more than four thousand recognised religions throughout the world, each with its own unique teaching and promise of an afterlife. But you may be surprised to learn that although religions play a vital part in the lives of so many people worldwide, in the spirit world—where all people come together—there is no one particular religion that everyone follows.

Many of us approach our religion as a sort of insurance policy. We may not be entirely convinced that there is a supreme being out there sitting in judgement of us, but we decide to follow a morally good life anyway . . . just in case.

Perhaps this is because most of us don't really have much choice in selecting our own religion. As a rule, we follow the religion that our parents followed and by the time we are old enough to consider other options and make up our own minds, life's demands have overtaken us and we don't bother. We stick with what we know, what is safe. Even if we no longer actively participate in our birth religion, we still carry its teachings with us. Consequently, this shapes the way we see the world and our place within it.

Our spiritual or religious leaning is almost always a product of our family history. It passes down from generation to generation. The values, principles and, dare we say, 'the commandments' of our family's religion are instilled within us from an early age. We watch our parents behave in a certain manner and accept this as the basis for our own moral and ethical code of life. Even atheists, who don't believe in God, still follow a set of rules based upon socially acceptable standards that have arisen largely from religious codes of conduct, though they may not care to admit it. If you ask an atheist if it is alright to steal or commit murder or adultery, most would say 'no'. Religious law has always been used to affirm useful moral laws in society.

The society, culture and time we are born into plays a significant part in our religious beliefs. If you are born in a mainly Christian country, you will most likely follow one of the Christian faiths, while someone born in an Islamic or Buddhist country will more than likely follow the religion of those countries. But religious and cultural practices also change over time. There was a time when it was against the law to be a Christian, and a time when people suspected of witchcraft were burned at the stake. The fact that we now find such intolerance outrageous is a product of the era we have been born into.

Humankind has never been able to agree on which religion is 'The One', but if we think about it logically, there cannot be only one spiritual pathway to eternity. If, for example, you believe in God, then you must by association believe that God created it all: every country, every culture, every religion, every person. Taking that thought process further, it stands to reason that because God is all powerful, then God must have got it right in the first place by creating such cultural and spiritual diversity.

When we asked Red Eagle his opinion on which religion best served humanity, he replied as a true sage would, giving a stunningly simple answer that raised even more questions: 'Surely our Creator did not build a flawed world.' That is the way of spirit guides. They are an enigmatic lot. Still, it was a humbling insight from the heart of a wise and compassionate soul.

To assume that people are destined to miss out on being looked after when they die just because they were born in a different part of the world is not only spiritually wrong, it is arrogant. It is this type of thinking that has resulted in thousands of years of cultural war and religious persecution on this planet. Red Eagle has told us that this is one of the reasons that spirit guides are so keen to develop and promote good mediumship. Our work not only brings comfort and healing to those in need, but it also shows that religion is neither a pathway nor a hindrance to renewal in the afterlife. Spiritual progress is available to every soul, no matter where they are born or what they believe.

The beauty of freedom of spiritual expression in the spirit

world is that there is room for everyone. Believer or non-believer, there is a place for you to fit in. The spirit world has no discernable cultural, religious or geographical borders. It is like looking across a vast grassy plain and being able to see everything clearly. The view is unobstructed.

The cultural divisions so much a part of this world are irrelevant in the spirit world because there is no need for them. In spirit we recognise that we are each a piece of life's big puzzle. Stripped of the trappings of the physical we are all equally important—and equally unimportant. Crossing over, we soon learn that we are home, that we are all part of the same spiritual family. Our souls, having been in spirit many times before, begin recalling the time before we were born. *Ah, yes . . . we have been here before!* It all comes back to us. We are eternal. The fact we are alive in the spirit world proves it.

But just like going to a new country where it takes time to adjust to the language and culture, it also takes time to readjust to life in the spirit world. The average person spends approximately 70 years on earth. That is an awfully long time invested in becoming the person you are when you die. Shaped by the life experiences you have had, you see yourself not as an eternal being who has evolved through many lifetimes but as an independent person, unique and separate from everyone else. There is nothing wrong with that. On earth it is necessary to think that way. The labels we give ourselves define us as individuals and help us make sense of ourselves and others as well as our place in the world. It is part and parcel of surviving life on this planet.

By the time we die, we are so confident of who we are and

where we fit in, that to consider ourselves as anything else would be akin to admitting we had lived our life as a mistake. But of course it wasn't a mistake. It was a role we played, a life we were meant to fulfil. Because our spiritual and religious values play such a role in defining who we are and what we consider normal, we are treated gently upon arrival in the spirit realms and given time to detach from the life we have just left behind. We are welcomed into a world that is consistent with our expectations. There is nothing out of the ordinary, nothing to fear.

Imagine being a devout Muslim and finding Jesus at the gates of heaven when what you expected to see was the prophet Mohammed standing there with open arms to greet you? Naturally, it would be confusing. You might even think that you have been banished to hell. Or imagine being an atheist who spent a life time railing against those who believed in a supreme being, only to be confronted by God the moment you arrived in the afterlife? You could be excused for thinking that someone was playing a joke on you.

The spirit world is an expedient one and things happen relatively quickly, which is why it is often said that there is no such thing as time in the spirit world. It is a world where our thoughts determine what we see and experience. If we expect to see a Muslim world, we will. If we expect to see the Summerland of milk and honey, we will. If we expect to see a great void where we just float in an eternal nothingness, then that is exactly what we will experience.

Many years ago, one of Australia's most wealthy businessmen had a sudden heart attack and a near-death experience before being revived. When he was well enough to speak about his experience, he said that he had not seen anything at all during the brief period when he was clinically dead. 'There is nothing out there,' he stated boldly. 'It was exactly what I was expecting to see.'

Aside from not being physical, the ability to create the world we want to live in by holding that vision in our thoughts is the most fundamental difference between the two worlds. Perhaps the businessman had spent much of his life stepping on others on his way to amassing his great fortune and for him seeing nothing was safer than seeing . . . what? Heaven? Hell? A judgemental God? 'Nothing' was what he expected— or hoped—to see. He wasn't disappointed.

If you had spent a very long physical lifetime with strong beliefs only to die and abruptly discover that you are completely wrong, then the afterlife would be a terrible shock. For this reason, when we cross over we automatically access a world that is initially in keeping with our expectation and comfort level. By entering a world that is almost identical to our old one, we quickly settle into the world of non-physical form and continue our soul's journey. In time, it all adjusts around us and we barely notice that we have moved into a completely different stage of life as a spirit.

Change of ingrained spiritual or religious beliefs in the spirit world is a natural occurrence, much like the cycles of the moon or the changing of seasons. It occurs as we shed the shackles of the physical and accept the reality that we are all fundamentally the same. There is an inevitability about it and it is always for the greater good.

This spiritual reality was made clear to us when Michelle recently did a reading for a lady named Astrid. Astrid desperately wanted to contact her mother Joyce, who had died ten years ago. As soon as Michelle made the connection, Joyce conveyed that she had always loved her daughter even though their relationship had been difficult. During the reading, Joyce referred to Astrid as a rebel. Astrid explained through tears of relief that she and her mother had always argued about her mother's religion. When alive, Joyce had been a devout Jehovah's Witness, and Astrid had refused to be part of her church. 'None of it matters now,' said Joyce. 'You are my daughter and I am sorry that my religion got in the way.'

It is a beautiful illustration of the way our attitudes to religion change once we are in the spirit world. In the end, Joyce loved her daughter more than her church, but it took her own death and rebirth into the spirit world for her to realise it.

The spiritual journey of each soul is to return to the spirit world and bring back all that it has learned on earth. That is the fulfilment of each particular role we have played, the purpose of the lifetime we have just lived. In playing our part, we insert another small piece to the jigsaw puzzle to which we all belong, making the picture a little clearer—and hopefully the world a little better—for the souls who will follow us. This is what is meant by the phrase 'What we do for one we do for all.' Religion, spirituality or a complete lack of faith are all equally valuable pieces of the puzzle. The spirit world does not prize one piece more highly than another.

12
Afterlife reunions

Reunions in the afterlife serve a great healing purpose. When we die and pass through the veil between worlds, we are greeted by the familiar faces of those who crossed over before us. Sharing the experience with loved ones assists us in adjusting to our new surroundings and settling into life as a spirit. It also does something much more powerful: It teaches us that the death we have just experienced was not the end and we are still very much alive.

Life in the spirit world is not a brand new life starting again from scratch. It is a continuation of the same life we were already living before we crossed over. It is the next stage.

Many people find comfort in knowing that their loved ones will meet them in the spirit world. But for some people these reunions pose a more practical problem. Helen arrived at one of our presentations with a healthy scepticism about mediums. She had been persuaded to attend by her daughter, who had seen us work many times and felt it would be a good idea for her mother to experience contact with the spirit world. At 84 years of age and with her health failing, Helen cautiously found some comfort in the possibility that there was an afterlife but was not convinced that mediums could really communicate with the spirits of the dead.

Helen may have been surprised to learn that we actually agree with her. When asked how it is possible to communicate with the spirit of the dead, our answer is always the same: it is *not* possible to communicate with the spirit of the dead. Dead things can't communicate because they have lost the life force that sparked them into being in the first place. But it *is* possible to communicate with the spirit of the living and those in the spirit world are most definitely living. They just happen to be living elsewhere. That place is the spirit world, a thriving vibrant realm where life continues when it can no longer be sustained here on earth. Our souls are infinite. They exist in spiritual form before we are born into our physical bodies and will return to spirit when our bodies reach their expiry date—whenever that may be.

During the evening, a male spirit named William identified himself and told us that Helen's hot water heater had recently broken and she was in urgent need of a new one. Shocked, Helen confirmed that, the previous day, her hot water heater had in fact sprung a leak and flooded her laundry room. 'William was my first husband,' she stammered nervously. 'But . . . how does he know that?'

We explained to Helen that from time to time William

was able to look into her world from his new home in the spirit realms. They had spent many years together before their marriage soured and ended. Apparently, William still felt a connection to Helen and watched over her. 'Oh dear, that's not good,' she replied gravely. 'You mean he can still see me?'

Enjoying his moment of recognition, as well as being entertained by his former wife's mild embarrassment, William asked us to tell her that the spirit of a gentleman named Michael was also present that evening and wanted to convey his love too. 'Tell her that we will both be there to greet her when she eventually joins us,' William said, chuckling. 'Then once and for all we will see who is the better man!'

'Goodness!' Helen exclaimed when told of this. 'Michael was my second husband! Don't tell me they are over there together? They couldn't stand one another when they were alive. Oh dear, what am I in for?'

The audience erupted into laughter. Helen was genuinely surprised that her two former husbands had met up in the spirit world and were still vying for her affections. But what really shook her world was when William casually mentioned the name Bruce.

'Oh, now you have really done it!' she said, horrified but laughing. 'Bruce is my *current* husband! If I have to choose between the three of them when I die, then I'm not going!'

The prospect of having to choose between three husbands in the afterlife was a considerable problem for Helen, but not for the reasons we might think.

'Frankly, I don't want to spend eternity with any of them,' she confided after the show. 'My heart always belonged to

Ernie. He was my high school sweetheart and my first love but he died in a mine shaft collapse when I was only seventeen so we never got to be together. The men I married were all good men in their own way but they were not Ernie. It wasn't really fair on any of them. They were competing with a ghost, a girlish romantic dream that started when I was a bright-eyed teenager and lasted my entire life. I don't know if it's possible but I was hoping that when I die, Ernie and I could finally be together. That's not too much to ask, is it?'

It was a good question. Does the afterlife offer us the opportunity to rekindle lost love?

Although she had lived a full and adventurous life, Helen admitted that she had never been able to rid herself of old regrets and felt she had been unfairly cheated out of her destiny. The heartbreak she suffered when Ernie died had never fully healed. 'No matter what I did or who I married, I always felt like they were only caretakers of my heart until it could be returned to the one it was meant for,' she explained. 'Maybe that was just wishful thinking but even though I got on with life, I have always held on to that hope.'

Over the years, Helen's story has become a great spiritual lesson that we share with our students through our seminars. It is the perfect example of how people who share time on earth are reunited in the spirit world—even those we hoped we would be well rid of. Family, friends, ex-husbands are all there in heaven's melting pot. Somehow it works. The petty squabbles and fight for survival and stature that are such features of life on this planet seem to dissolve in the spirit realms. Many spirits have told us that the arguments they had with people while here on earth were quickly and easily resolved in the afterlife. Reawakening to our true spiritual nature helps us see that we are all part of the same spiritual family. The life roles we have just played were part of our soul's growth and learning experience.

The idea that real love never dies is a deliciously enticing one. Our students always enjoy the story about Helen. Would she meet up with Ernie, her true love, and rekindle a romance that had been cruelly cut short all those years ago? Did she have a choice in the matter? It was a scenario that led to many insightful discussions and theories. Of course, we couldn't know for sure how it all panned out . . . or could we?

Several years later a middle-aged woman named Beryl came to see us for a private reading. During the session, a beautiful light started shining into the room which seemed to make the veil between worlds translucent. It was as if a portal had been deliberately opened through space and time so we could look inside and witness for ourselves exactly what happened in the spirit world. We told Beryl what we were seeing.

'There are two rows of people forming a guard of honour,' Michelle said. 'They are clapping and cheering, welcoming a woman into their world. That woman is your mother.

'The people forming the guard of honour are all people she knows. Your mum is smiling from ear to ear. She is very happy to see them all. There is a man named William who seems to be acting like a host or master of ceremonies. He is inviting her to walk through the guard of honour. As she passes through it, each face stands out more clearly. They are all people who have died before her.

'She walks through the guard of honour and acknowledges all the well-wishers until she gets to the end where she sees a handsome young man standing there bathed in the most brilliant light imaginable. He is holding a baby in his arms. It is a boy. The woman is crying now, but they are tears of joy. She is so happy to see him. It's like everyone is getting out of her way so that she can be with the young man and the baby. They were all expecting her and knew this moment was coming. William is telling her that everything will be okay. He is pointing towards the young man holding the baby and telling her that it is alright for her to go to them.'

Beryl sobbed softly and needed a few moments to compose herself. There was no rush. We were being given a rare treat, a glimpse into an afterlife reunion where friends and family had gathered to welcome home one of their own.

'You probably don't remember,' Beryl said, 'but a few years ago my mother and I came along to one of your shows and Mum received a message from her first husband, my father William, as well as her second husband Michael. She was the lady who worried about which husband she would have to spend eternity with.'

'Your mum is Helen!' we exclaimed simultaneously.

Until that moment we hadn't recognised Beryl. We see thousands of people a year through our private and public sessions and while many of their stories stay with us afterwards, most simply fade away. This inability to recall the detail of every reading is a protective mechanism put in place by our spirit guides. It ensures that we are not emotionally or mentally burned out by the enormous energy needed to work as full-time mediums and teachers. (Well, that is our excuse for being so horribly forgetful anyway!) In our light-hearted moments, we sometimes refer to this as 'psychic amnesia' or 'brain drain'!

We explained this to Beryl and said that while we may have forgotten their faces, Helen made quite an impression on us. Beryl laughed when we told her we have shared her mother's story many times and how it always brought both humour and understanding.

Then Beryl revealed: 'After that night at your show, Mum was so worried about having to choose between Dad and the others that she started crying when we got home. I didn't know how to console her. I told her not to worry, that many women had more than one husband and that I was sure that somehow it would all work out. That's when she told me about Ernie. Apparently she met him when she was seventeen and they were deeply in love. They were planning on getting married.'

Remembering the conversation with Helen all those years ago, we told Beryl that her mother had also told us about Ernie. 'I'm sorry that we upset her,' Ezio said.

'Don't be,' Beryl replied. 'Mum was always a worrier. She worried about who she would end up with when she died. But that night we shared the most intimate conversation. We were always close but after your show we really connected. I think Mum found something in your message that let her dare to dream that maybe—just maybe—she would see Ernie again. Then she told me a secret that she had never told anyone. I don't know how she lived with it all those years.

'When Ernie died in that mine accident, Mum was pregnant with his baby. But the trauma she experienced because of his death caused her to miscarry. No one knew. Not her parents, not her friends . . . no one. She suffered silently her entire life. The part that hurt her the most was that Ernie only went to work in the mines to earn some extra money for a deposit on a house. He had asked Mum to marry him. It was the happiest time of her life. Then it was all taken away. She was only seventeen.

'You don't know what it means to me to know that she is finally reunited with Ernie and her baby.'

Helen's story, along with many others we have witnessed over the years, is a touching one. It shows us that there is always something to look forward to in the afterlife and reminds us once again that love never dies.

PART FOUR

Living in the Spirit World

13
T.J.'s view from above

We were having a rare night off, relaxing in our lounge room and watching television, when a sudden swirl of purple and blue light appeared in the far corner of the room. It was T.J.

When a spirit wishes to make a physical appearance, there needs to be a shift in the electromagnetic field that separates their world from ours. This shift enables them to generate a 'form' that is more visible to the naked eye—especially if that eye is trained to see them. A great deal of effort is required to pierce through the veil in this way and it takes the combined effort of many spirits to generate enough spiritual power to make it happen. That is why materialisations are not often used to convey messages from those in the afterlife. It is too labour intensive and the image can only be projected for a very short period.

For the most part, regular spirit communication takes place through what is referred to as mental mediumship, which simply means that the medium and the spirit have connected mind to mind—or telepathically. Mental mediumship is the most common form of communicating with the spirit world. It is more efficient than materialisation because it requires fewer spirits and less energy to effect the communication.

Because it is unusual, a medium knows to pay particular attention when a materialisation occurs. T.J. could have simply called out his message in the usual way, but by manifesting in our lounge room in a dramatic swirl of colour and light, he was much more likely to make us notice. This particular evening, the young man had rallied enough friends and family in the spirit world to make sure he got through.

'My mum has seen the same colour when I'm around,' he stated proudly. 'She caught it in a photograph and put it on Facebook! Some of our friends don't really think it is me. They think it's just a reflection of light off the camera lens. They are wrong. I can make an impression sometimes, like the time I was able to flare the garage light so Dad could see it. He kept asking me to do more but I couldn't. I know he was disappointed.

'Mum gets upset that it doesn't happen often enough but the longer I'm over here, the harder it is to do. It's not that I don't want to appear in pictures. I always loved having my photo taken. But it's as if I'm moving away from being physical. My body—or the power it used to have—doesn't exist anymore. I'm still me but it's harder to make my presence felt down there. Make sure you tell her that. Tell her not to be sad because of it. I'm always around and I know how much they love me and miss me. It's just that I'm pure spirit now. Like I'm electricity. They can't see me . . . but I'm always there. Make sure you tell her that the blue and purple lights are me. She really is the orb lady!'

Then T.J. said: 'I've come here because I want you to tell Mum that I don't have a problem with him being convicted for manslaughter instead of murder.'

We made a mental note to do as T.J. had asked. The next day, before we got around to contacting her, Christine sent the following email:

So the murderer wants to plead manslaughter. We have an opportunity to put across our views and opinions.

I feel that if we don't accept it, we will go to trial and there's a slim chance that he could walk away free and clear. All it takes is one goody-two-shoes on the jury feeling sorry for the guy.

If we accept the manslaughter plea, he will definitely do time but with a reduced sentence.

I feel guilty of betraying T.J. if I accept the manslaughter plea. But it would save T.J.'s friends from being dragged over the coals in the witness stand, and my family the pain of T.J.'s name being dragged through the mud. It could make the killer look more innocent and T. J. look feral and guilty.

I am frightened of disappointing him. Should I just continue the fight and strive for the biggest charge?

I know you are not my personal counsellors but I am so mixed up about which road to take and I do value your opinion . . . and I know you can hear him and I can't. So, when you're chatting with my son, can you try and ask him if I am doing the right thing? Please help.

Christine

After receiving her email, we immediately called Christine and told her that T.J. had visited us the night before and said that he was satisfied with a manslaughter charge being laid against his killer as opposed to a murder charge. Privately, we were glad T.J. had pushed through the veil between worlds and made his feelings known. Not only did it remove the heavy responsibility from his mum and dad's shoulders but it removed it from ours. Whenever spirits use a form of physical phenomenon to break through the veil and grab our attention, it means that they don't want to be misinterpreted. By literally turning up to tell us his message, T.J. didn't have to risk us giving his mum an inaccurate psychic interpretation of what he thought about the lesser plea. The words came directly from him. There could be no mistake.

At the time he came to us, T.J.'s comment didn't really make any sense because we were not aware that his killer would have an option to face anything *other* than a murder charge. After Christine's email, it made perfect sense.

'I just don't want it to drag on forever,' Christine said over the phone. 'As long as the killer gets a reasonable period in jail, then I think it's worth avoiding the risk of him getting let off on a technicality or some other stupid thing. But then I worry that T.J. might think that we are not fighting hard enough for him. Do you know what I mean?'

We knew exactly what she meant and so did T.J. Visiting us the night before Christine sent her email was his proactive way of showing that he already knew of the dilemma his family would soon be facing. He knew that a decision loomed that would cause great distress among those he loved, and he was trying to save his family the trauma of a full judicial trial. By accepting a manslaughter plea, they were finally putting the legal matter to rest—even though they would still have to contend with losing their only son for the rest of their lives.

In some of our past dealings, T.J. had shown a willingness to try to influence proceedings, telling us that from time to time he was able to whisper a suggestion into the ears of investigating officers to make them follow certain leads or clues in the pursuit of his assailants. It appeared that by letting everyone know that he was fine with his family agreeing to a lesser plea than the one they originally expected, he was attempting to influence matters in this instance too. The charge of manslaughter carries a lesser jail sentence than one of murder because it recognises that the person who committed the crime did not intentionally set out to end the victim's life. T.J. knew that his killer did not mean to kill him even though having a knife in his possession spelt trouble from the outset—especially because T.J. himself had been unarmed.

From what he had previously told us, T.J. knew that his stabbing was just a stupid act that happened during a few minutes of madness as he tried to prevent a group of angry young men from attacking his friend. But he also knew that his family needed a resolution as part of their healing process.

Christine and Todd were walking a fine line between legal expediency and justice. Their son knew that they needed a break from the constant strain that was tearing them apart.

Sadly, that's where T.J.'s plan came unstuck. A week or so later, Christine emailed again, letting us know that they had rejected the manslaughter charge:

> The prosecutor said that if we agreed to that rat's guilty plea to manslaughter instead of murder, the most he would get would be four years in jail. Four years!
>
> With time served pending his trial, that means he will be out in a couple of years. He will only be 23 when he gets out of jail with his whole life ahead of him. Young enough so that maybe one day he could have a wife and children of his own. T.J. never made it to seventeen. My son's life is worth so much more than that.
>
> Todd said, 'That's crap! We're not agreeing to that!' This time he was the vocal one and I just sat there in stunned silence as the deputy public prosecutor [DPP] laid out all the scenarios.
>
> The DPP said it was a joke too. If pleading to manslaughter, gave him, say, ten or twelve years in jail, then we would have agreed to it. It is a penalty that makes a difference . . . but four years with recognition of time already served while he awaits his trial? It's just not on! That's the legal system for you. We are going into battle for our boy.

Although he had frequently shown an exceptional ability to look into the lives of his parents and sisters and recount all manner of current happenings in great detail, being a spirit didn't suddenly make T.J. infallible.

'I didn't see that coming,' he said in a tone that didn't hide his dismay. 'I thought for sure that even if he pleaded guilty to manslaughter he would get a longer sentence. He deserves it. Not so much for what he did to me . . . but for what he has done to my family. You kind of lose perspective over here. Maybe Mum and Dad do need to fight. Maybe that's what will get them through all this. It's in our blood anyway . . . we have always been a family of fighters. It's who we are.'

Many people think that dying makes us all-knowing but we don't magically acquire the wisdom of Solomon when we enter the spirit world. By and large we are still the same person we were before crossing over and, in the short term at least, our personalities dictate how we respond to events that unfold. Sometimes, the elevated vista from the spirit world can give us a bird's-eye view of what is happening down below on earth and we can better judge what is about to happen. But it is not seeing the future. It is seeing what is logically due to happen next. It's like flying high above the ground in a helicopter, looking down on the world below. From up high you can see further than you could if you were on the ground— but you still can't see everything.

Being part of the spirit world removes us from much of the grind of daily life and our decision-making process is influenced by the higher ideals of compassion, love and forgiveness. The deep insight and healing this brings means that emotions such as anger, hurt and the need for revenge all dissipate quickly into the ether. A spirit can easily lose sight of what it takes to heal here on earth. They can sometimes misjudge the amount of time and effort it takes for their loved ones to complete the grieving cycle.

As it turned out, T.J. had not misjudged the situation at all. He had not been trying to influence his parents' decision to fight or accept a manslaughter plea for his assailant. Nor was he predicting the outcome. He just wanted to give them options they could live with. From his vantage point in the spirit world, he could see the bigger picture and was trying to let his family know that whatever path they chose to walk through the legal minefield, he was walking right along with them.

Later, T.J. told us that now that he was in the spirit world, what happened to his killer didn't really matter to him. 'I see it a bit differently now, that's for sure,' he said, referring to his killer. 'I know that we sort of had some involvement together before we were born and that he was always going to end up doing me in. Maybe that's the way it was planned—I'm not sure yet.'

But he knew that it mattered to his family. 'I don't need justice for myself,' he said solemnly. 'I just need it for everyone else. Mum, Dad, Rhiannon and Teigen are all hurting. They need something. I think we have to fight. No one will be happy if we don't. Tell Mum and Dad that I am ready to fight with them. They don't have to do it on their own. Win, lose or draw, it won't matter . . . it's the right thing to do.'

T.J. understood his family's struggle to rebuild their lives. 'Everything we do is overshadowed by T.J.'s death,' Christine said sadly. 'Those bastards took away everything. I know that we still have two beautiful daughters and that their lives still count for something, but it's just so hard to get past it. I just miss him so much.'

When confronted by tragedy, each family member deals with the fallout in their own way. Some, like Christine, find their voice through Facebook, where she vents and surrounds herself with loving memories and supporters of her son, taking brief moments of comfort where she can find them. Others, like her husband Todd, want to crawl into a deep dark hole and shield their broken heart away from the rest of the world.

T.J. was acutely aware of what his family was going through. 'Even just seeing my friends playing football down at the park is enough to bring about a real downer for Dad,' he told us. T.J.'s beloved football club had recently announced a perpetual shield for courage and commitment to be awarded each year in his honour. 'Okay, so losing me is hard on all of them. But at least I get an award named after me,' T.J. joked in an effort to convince his parents that the boy they loved was still just as brash and cheeky as ever. 'Every year, someone who shows that they are not afraid to put their body on the line for their team will be honoured in my name. I am an immortal now!'

T.J. had never been one to sit back and let a bad situation unfold—not if he thought he could make it better. That was just his way. He had been trying to protect his family within the framework of what he could see happening. Now, circumstances had changed. His family needed him to stand alongside them. Come what may, he would support and defend his 'crew'.

'It was precisely that attitude that got him killed,' Christine said with a sigh when we told her that her son would be with them through thick and thin. 'Still, that's who he was. You have got to love him for it.'

Christine didn't say as much but we could tell that, despite the twists and turns, she was relieved that the decision had finally been made. She could now focus on getting justice for her son. Like a lioness preparing to defend her cub, she too was ready for the fight.

14
Astral travel

In spiritual circles, people often talk of the astral planes and astral travel. It all sounds very exotic with its implication of floating free among the heavens and stars or visiting faraway places that you might never be able to go to in ordinary life. Of course, there's more to it than that.

Astral travel occurs when our spirit temporarily leaves our body. This is possible because our spirit is not locked into our physical body. Astral travel happens in one of two ways: intentionally through the practice of meditation as we seek spiritual enlightenment, or naturally while we are asleep.

Sometimes, during sleep, our spirit leaves our body so it can replenish itself in its purest state without the effort of holding on to human form. It returns before we awake and usually we are none the wiser, although we may sometimes remember parts of what happened while we were 'out there' in the form of a dream.

Waking suddenly with a start can sometimes be a result of our spirit returning to our bodies from the astral planes where we have been roaming. Our spirit is connected to our body by an etheric lifeline known as the silver cord. The silver cord is a safety feature that ensures our soul never separates completely from our bodies and remains in the spirit world. It is like an astronaut's lifeline when they space-walk. It stretches from our physical body, lying fast asleep in bed, to our spirit or 'astral body' which is out doing what it needs to do. Occasionally, something happens that makes the silver cord snap back too quickly like an elastic band that has been fully stretched and then released. The sudden return is vigorous enough to startle us awake.

Many people have spoken to us of waking abruptly and feeling as though they are paralysed for a few moments. Those who experience this can find it very frightening and some believe they have been pinned down by a 'bad' spirit. It is important to reassure them that this is not the case. We explain that they have woken before their spirit has fully settled back into their body. There is protection in place which immobilises our body while our spirit is roaming free. This ensures that our body is not capable of getting out of bed and walking around endangering itself without its spirit being present.

Our mind is the gateway to the astral plane, which is why meditation and sleep work so well in helping us go there. During meditation or sleep, our mind is less busy and not actively involved in other day-to-day activities. It is able to be a doorway to spiritual realms rather than being a controller for our regular life functions. This is why we use meditation as the primary tool in helping our students develop their own mediumistic abilities. It trains them to keep their own thoughts out of the way so they can receive messages from spirit.

The astral realm has many levels and serves several purposes. The lower plane works as a buffer between worlds while the higher planes are where we receive healing, spiritual tuition, reunion with loved ones and a return to the Creator.

The lower astral plane is the part of the spirit realm that is closest to us because it consists of denser energy and vibrates at a slower rate than the rest of the spirit world. Its function is to separate our physical world from the non-physical one. The lower astral plane acts as a barrier between these worlds and is literally the 'veil' referred to by spiritualists and mystics.

Every thought and emotion we project during our earthly life generates energy that has to go somewhere, and the lower astral plane is where it all ends up. Being closest to earth, it also absorbs and/or filters much of the residual energy of all living things that pass through it. When we die, we pass through the lower astral plane on our way to our initial resting place in spirit.

The lower astral plane is a repository or warehouse for human experience and therefore similar to our world. It is the easiest plane to connect to psychically. Many students starting out on their psychic or mediumistic development connect quickly to the lower astral plane and convince themselves that they are far more developed than they really are because information from there comes through so readily.

Because the lower astral plane holds all the leftover commotion of the physical world, it can be a very confusing place. This is why it is necessary to keep it separate from the physical world. All the mental and emotional energy we send out both consciously and subconsciously swirls around in an invisible holding pattern and there seems to be no logical order to it. The lower astral plane is noisy and chaotic.

Imagine you are walking down the street and each time you pass someone, a snippet of their thoughts, feelings or desires rushes into your mind. You are hearing words and feeling emotions that are random and scattered and make no sense. Each bit of information is real but together they're incoherent. It is just noise and might go something like this: *Oh, I want that job so badly I am a nervous wreck about the interview . . . Wow! My world is just perfect today . . . I hope he proposes soon . . . It's so crowded here I feel sick . . . Should I buy that blue dress? . . . Oh, my head hurts! . . . Well, I hope she is happy with herself now! . . .* To make matters worse, each of these disjointed statements is accompanied by a different face and a rush of the emotion they are feeling.

Of course, you would feel dizzy, bombarded, upset, and wish it would all just stop! This is what many people who suffer psychosis and some other forms of mental illness experience. There is a tear or damage to their aura which results in their minds being open to the lower astral plane—all the time. It must be exhausting.

As mediums, we train ourselves to rise above the psychic layers of noise and confusion to connect to the spirits relevant to those who seek our help. For this reason, we are very strict about when we open up to the spirit world. We don't just walk around all day giving each other messages. More importantly, we don't walk around giving messages to other people. Being disciplined stops us being overwhelmed in the manner we have just described and protects our own auras from wear and tear.

Leaving the door between worlds constantly ajar is a dangerous practice. It leads to mental and emotional burnout. Because we value what we do and want to continue working for the spirit world for many years to come, we try to conscientiously follow the guidelines our spirit helpers have set down for us: open to spirit when we're working; don't open when we're not. There are of course times when spirits make their presence known even when we aren't working, however, such as the time T.J. visited us on our night off.

When doing readings there must be a spiritual contract in place to avoid tapping into the lower astral realm. A reading must be requested by the person who wants it, or else that spiritual contract does not exist. Be very cautious of any person who approaches you and attempts to give you a reading without being asked. Though such people may be well intentioned, they are keeping themselves open to the lower astral plane. Randomly opening up to the astral plane is akin to opening the front door of your house and inviting any stranger to come in and make themselves at home. You wouldn't put yourself or your family at risk like that. It is best to use the same discretion with spirits.

The lower astral plane serves an important purpose for those of us in the physical world and an equally important purpose for those who have crossed over. When the spirit leaves the body, its vibration rapidly increases as it leaves behind the heaviness of physical life. T.J. illustrated this brilliantly when describing his transition—it is that feeling he had of heightened senses, sharp awareness of everything around him from the grass and insects to the birds sleeping in the trees. He was aware of their life force . . . their spirit.

Under normal circumstances those who are crossing over make a clean break, and as their vibration increases on leaving this world, they pass briefly through the lower astral plane on their journey. It is entirely probable that the lower astral plane is the tunnel that so many who have had a near-death experience describe. It is most likely where the commonly used terms for dying such as 'crossing over' and 'passing over' originated, because we literally cross or pass through this plane, the veil that separates the two worlds—the 'other side' is the other side of the lower astral plane.

Like T.J., the majority of people who cross over will barely notice they are passing through the lower astral plane. He describes the sensation of leaving his body, the realisation that he is dying, and then very quickly his grandmother and uncle are there with him, both to comfort him and to confirm beyond doubt his suspicion that he is leaving his earthly life behind. Their presence reassures him that although he has physically died, his spirit is still very much alive. The very nature of a soul's journey means passing through the lower astral plane, but it is worth noting that although T.J. was killed and left the earth suddenly, there was not even the faintest suggestion that his soul was trapped there—not even for a moment.

T.J., his grandmother and uncle, like most spirits who have crossed over, do not live in the lower astral plane. They pass through it and then settle into their place in the spirit world along with those who have previously made the journey or who are preparing to return for another life. There are those, however, who may choose to stay in the lower astral plane for a time. As we have said previously, the journey of each soul is an individual one and personal choice plays a role. In Chapter 8, 'Lost passports and misplaced souls', we explained some of the reasons why an individual may choose not to enter the realms of spirit immediately. Those who decide to remain close to the earth plane reside in the lower astral plane, amid the noise and confusion where they can dwell for as long as they choose. Once again, it is important to realise that they are not trapped or lost but have made a decision to stay there. As soon as they decide that the time is right, they will be welcomed into the spirit world to continue their soul's journey.

Astral travel is not a chance occurrence. We all travel through the lower astral plane when we die. But we also travel through there many times during our earthly lives. Whether through the practice of meditation or during sleep, we astral travel for a variety of reasons and our spirits are safe. Sometimes we will meet with our departed loved ones for a brief hello, a reassurance that they are okay. Sometimes our spirit needs some healing and will stretch out along its silver cord to receive it. For those who work with spirit or are developing their abilities as mediums, spirit guides and helpers will regularly meet us in the higher astral planes to teach us what we need to learn.

Even if we do not remember these journeys upon waking, they remain with us on a deeply emotional level—a soul level. The teachings we have shared in become part of the fabric of our being. While our physical body rests, our spirit has been busy. So, next time you are out roaming the astral realms, don't be afraid. We wish you safe and happy travels!

15
Caring for kids in spirit

Parents don't expect to outlive their children. The enduring heartache of losing a child is something we pray that none of us ever has to bear. Not that long ago, we attended the university graduation of Michelle's younger sister Siobhan. It was a proud moment for all the family. During the presentation ceremony, Michelle's mother leaned over and whispered proudly, 'I made that.'

It was a sentiment that many of us who have given birth to or raised children can easily identify with. We feel both pride and satisfaction when we watch the children we love make their own way in the world. The pain a parent feels in their heart when their child dies must be excruciating— no matter how old that child might be. Whether the child was five, fifteen or 50—being alive when they are gone is a heartbreak that most parents never really recover from. The expectation is that we should outlive our offspring. It isn't always the case.

Shelley was a fit, healthy 28-year-old woman when she was diagnosed with a rare form of adrenal cancer. Ironically, the disease only came to light after she was hit by a car while riding her pushbike along a busy suburban street. During her convalescence from the accident, Shelley inexplicably began gaining a concerning amount of weight. The doctors were baffled. They assumed that her rapid weight gain was due to an enforced lack of activity as she recovered from her injuries. They didn't suspect that a seemingly healthy young woman like Shelley had an aggressive tumour growing inside her.

Her parents, Don and Marion, told us that even though they were devastated by the news of Shelley's cancer, their daughter was such a strong and beautiful force of nature that no one really expected the illness to take her life. Everyone, including Shelley, believed she would beat it.

'I only wish I had said more . . . done more,' Marion lamented. 'In those situations you just try to stay positive and not talk about what is happening . . . or what *could* happen. We didn't want to tempt fate by bringing our fear of losing her out into the open. But now I think that there was so much more that I could have—or should have—said. The entire family was so relieved that she wasn't killed in the bike accident, only to be shattered by the news that she had cancer. We just couldn't believe it. Six years after her death I still can't believe it. She was so beautiful, so young and vital.

'Everyone loved Shelley. She was always such an active, happy person with a lot of energy and time for others. After she was diagnosed with cancer, she became involved with Relay for Life, which is an annual fundraiser for the Cancer Council. It is a 24-hour relay where people walk or run or ride bikes around an athletic field and raise funds that go to cancer research and support groups. It has a real community atmosphere where people like us who lost their loved ones to cancer get together and, well, it's sad but uplifting at the same time. All the families and friends—we all know what the others have been through. It does help.

'Our local branch is one of the largest in the country and we are still actively involved in all the organising and fundraising. They now have a memorial trophy in Shelley's honour which is just wonderful.' Marion's voice wavered as she added, 'I know that she would love the fact we're still involved. That's why we do it.'

Don and Marion are also wonderful supporters of our work and regularly attend our public shows, as well as private readings. 'We always want Shelley to come through, of course,' Marion once told us, 'but we are not disappointed when she doesn't. We are both just as happy when other people get messages too. We love coming along to the shows and being part of the healing they bring. To see people's reactions when you prove that their loved ones are still around just warms my heart. All those personal details you give them make such a world of difference.'

Over the years, Shelley has made contact through our mediumship many times, delivering unique and often quirky validations that she is watching over her family and actively participating in their daily lives. She has mentioned handwritten notes placed in her coffin by her parents and brother, as well as a teddy bear that was placed alongside her by a dear family friend named Kris. Most of all, Shelley appears to enjoy telling her family things that they don't yet know, so she can experience their surprise and delight when she, and ultimately we, are proven correct.

One time, Shelley told us that she had seen her brother, Stuart, standing in his front yard and looking at the new cracks which had just appeared in his concrete driveway. Stuart confirmed that the event Shelley described had in fact taken place only a few days earlier. On the same night, she also connected with her cousin who was in the audience by mentioning that she recently saw her drop a jar of maple syrup on the kitchen floor. Shelley chuckled sympathetically as she recounted the sticky gooey mess that had to be cleaned up as a consequence.

On another occasion during a private session, Shelley spoke lovingly of her young niece Maddison. Shelley told us that Maddison had been complaining that her mother was putting too much Vegemite on her sandwiches and that it had irritated her mouth. Marion laughed when this information was relayed to her but she didn't really believe it because, like many Australian kids, Maddison loved her Vegemite. Marion said she would check with her daughter-in-law Jane, Maddison's mother, and get back to us.

Because she had experienced our work many times before, Marion knew that information often came through that needed someone else to validate it. By delivering messages containing information that needs more people to validate its accuracy, the spirit world is able to spread their message of life after death even further than would otherwise be possible. Our guides often refer to this phenomenon as spiritual networking, which is a neat way of saying that they just love getting their afterlife message out to as many people as possible. Over the years, we have noticed that they are exceptionally good at it. Shelley was good at it too. By mentioning the Vegemite story, she knew it would engage other family members who were not present that day. She was getting her message out there. Although no longer part of this world, she was always part of those she loved.

The next day, Marion emailed us. 'Well, you were right again!' she conceded happily. 'After the reading, I called Jane and asked her about it. Apparently Maddison came home from school *that very day* and complained that her mother had spread too much Vegemite on her sandwich and it had burned her mouth! Jane couldn't believe it. It brings us so much comfort to know that Shelley is watching over her niece.'

Such experiences have taught us the importance of spiritual networking. It is the spirit world's way of bringing more people into the loop. In this case, not only had Shelley been able to make contact with her mother during a private sitting, she was also able to connect with her sister-in-law Jane and, of course, her young niece Maddison. Three people for the price of one—most definitely a spiritual bargain! Shelley is clearly a loving soul. She, like others who have crossed over into the spirit world, knows that her family still need her around.

Demonstrating such intimate detail about the ordinary lives of her family proves that Shelley is watching over them. It's the type of information that we refer to as 'proof of consciousness'—proof that not only are our loved ones present in the afterlife, but that they are able to peer through the veil between worlds and learn what is happening in the lives of those they left behind. Proof of consciousness simply means that the spirit still has active intelligence. It is an incredibly important aspect of mediumship because it brings comfort to our clients when we are able to prove that their loved ones know things that are currently happening in their lives. It shows that they are nearby.

Perhaps the most striking Shelley moment came the day before we began writing this chapter, when she unexpectedly visited us at home and suggested that she, rather than anyone else, was the best spirit to enlighten us about what happens to children in the spirit world. 'Shelley really loved children,' her father Don once told us. 'She was always queen of the kids. They just flocked to her.'

On numerous occasions during our public readings, we have been aware of a strong female presence gathering up children in spirit who wish to connect with their parents in the audience, showing them how to get our attention. She showed the children where to stand, how to project images into our minds, and how to transmit their voices so we could hear them. That female presence is Shelley and we love it when she comes to work with us. One night, she helped us connect to a young girl who had died from spina bifida. The girl's sister later told us that her sibling had been unable to speak when she was alive. Shelley helped the child find her spiritual voice so she could let her sister know how much she appreciated all that had been done for her. Another time she helped a young man who had taken his own life find the right words to tell his mother he was sorry. It was an extremely emotional moment for everyone present, including us.

That she would wish to be part of this chapter is not surprising because Shelley has regularly shown her fondness for working with spirit children. What is surprising, however, is her delightful sense of timing. The day she contacted us to offer her service was her mother's birthday! Her involvement in *Postcards from the Other Side* is Shelley's birthday gift to her mum.

'Children in the spirit world are always looked after,' Shelley explained. 'When they die, they are instantly reunited with family members who are already here. Sometimes they know the people they meet and sometimes they don't. But they are never afraid. There is something within our soul that recognises our family when we cross over. It's instant. There is little or no time lag between dying and being connected to your family. Everyone is safe.

'Kids are never left unattended. Anyone with bad intentions can't get near them so no parent ever need worry. Because kids are so pure and innocent, they are on an entirely different wavelength to everyone else. It's like they are on different planets. Even kids who think that they have done something wrong and want to hide are still protected and given time to adjust. There is no pressure put on anyone over here, especially not children.'

Over the years we have conducted countless readings for parents grieving the loss of children. In every case, the first thing that these parents want to know is that their child is well and looked after in the spirit world. Shelley's observation that the innocence of children serves as a protective mechanism in the spirit world has not only been confirmed by our spirit guides, but by other spirits who have been able to clearly explain this phenomenon over the years. We are grateful to all of them for helping us understand what happens to children when they die.

A spirit called Ralph once came through during a reading and asked us to tell his niece Lisa that her son Braddon was in a 'separate mind space' from his father in the spirit world. This proved to be a great source of comfort to Lisa because, tragically, Braddon was murdered by his own father. 'He can't get to your baby, Lisa,' Ralph said. 'They are in different places.'

For people to come together in the spirit world they must be of like heart and mind. This means that until spirits have received any healing they require, or made appropriate reparations, they reside in a different place from others who are more innocent, such as children. This is a naturally occurring protective mechanism in the afterlife. We have never witnessed the suffering of children in the spirit world.

The ease with which we are able to connect to our friends and family in the afterlife when we cross over is reassuring. If people of like mind and like heart want to be together in the afterlife, it is simply a matter of concentrating on it.

Roger survived a horrific car accident only to discover that his two daughters had not. Initially, the girls appeared reluctant to communicate with their father. Although the coroner ruled that the car crash was an unfortunate accident and no one was to blame, Roger understandably assumed his daughters' reluctance to communicate was because they blamed him for their death.

Eventually the eldest girl told us that they were together and happy in the spirit world and that they did not blame their father for their tragic passing. Instead, they were worried that their father had been contemplating suicide to be with them—or, if truth be told—in a misguided attempt to atone for their deaths. They didn't want to make the afterlife sound like an attractive proposition for their dad. 'He won't end up in the same place if he commits suicide,' she warned. 'Tell him to promise that he will stay there with Mum.'

The girls knew that if their father took his own life his mental anguish would have resulted in him being in a different place to them. Obviously Roger is not a bad person, but the manner of his death would temporarily keep him in a different spiritual place to his daughters. If he committed suicide he would need ongoing healing to deal with his actions and their consequences before a reunion could take place.

Roger cried when we told him what they had said, but he did promise his daughters to fight his pain and not take his own life. He also agreed to seek grief counselling, which seemed to satisfy his girls, making them more chatty.

Shelley explained to us that some kids who die young seem to grow faster than they would have if they were still on earth. 'I think this is because they will eventually become like guardian angels for their family members,' she said. 'These kids seem a bit different to the others. Maybe they are what you would call "old souls". They may have been young in earthly terms but are spiritually wise. It's beautiful to watch how their love transforms the people they care for. On earth, we don't realise just how the love of those in spirit shapes our destiny. And no one loves more honestly than children.

'But most kids choose to grow in the spirit world at the same rate they would have grown if they were still on earth. If you ask them what they want, most say they want to be with their family. So they are allowed to grow in a life parallel to the one their families are living. They know about their brothers and sisters, their cousins and friends. They learn things the same as they would have if they were still at school, and play games with other kids, just like they would on earth.

'But is not really school like you would know it. In spirit, the value of love is the greatest lesson we ever learn.'

There are many special souls who dedicate their time in the afterlife to helping recently crossed over children acclimatise to their new surroundings. Shelley is one such soul. 'I have tried a lot of things since I have been over here,' she said. 'But working with and helping children is what really inspires me. I love it.'

From our earliest meetings with Marion, Don and Shelley, it was obvious that the young woman had a burning desire to work with children in the afterlife. During one particular session she drew our attention to a number of bald children in the spirit world who were happily laughing and cheering, waving head scarves and coloured bandanas in the air to attract our attention. It was obvious that all these children had died of cancer. Shelley revealed that she had taken on a type of counsellor's role in the afterlife, bringing them together for some fun and laughter.

'Their short lives were so filled with horrible things like pain and chemotherapy—I just wanted to help them enjoy kids' stuff for a change,' Shelley told us. 'I'm not the only one. There are lots of people over here who dedicate their time to helping children. It doesn't take much to put the sparkle back in their eyes.'

'I'm not surprised,' Marion said when we relayed this. 'When she was sick, Shelley always said that she wanted to help the kids in the Starlight Foundation, which is a charity that gives terminally ill children a chance to fulfil a wish, like a trip to Disneyland or meeting their favourite sportsperson. She said that there was always someone worse off than she was. I don't know where she found that strength. But she got too sick and didn't get around to it.'

'She always cared so much for others,' Marion continued, tears welling in her eyes. 'One day we were having lunch at a local cafe when one of Shelley's friends came by. She was all excited about a holiday she was planning and they talked for ages. When the girl left, I asked Shelley why she didn't tell her friend that she was sick. She smiled and said, "Mum, she was so excited about her holiday that I didn't want to ruin it for her." My heart just broke. I looked at her and said, "Shelley . . . have I ever told you how much I love you?"'

16
Soul groups— Companions on the trip of a lifetime

When we are born into this world, we temporarily forget our spiritual family but that does not mean that some of them are not here travelling with us. While we often have close and loving ties with our soul group members on earth, our relationships with them are not always easy—sometimes they are here to present us with challenges too. This combination of positive and negative influences throughout our lives helps us to learn and grow.

There is a wonderful saying that people come into your life for a reason, a season or a lifetime. This is certainly the way it works with members of your soul group. Some are here for the long haul, standing by you through thick and thin.

Others play more temporary roles that shape your destiny by nudging your life in a different direction to the one it was taking. All are equally valid.

Ruth, a well-spoken lady in her mid-fifties, came to us for a reading hoping to make a connection with her mum who had passed several years earlier. The reading began and Ruth was shocked to the core when the first spirit to communicate was not her mother, but an old teacher—a very strict Catholic nun called Sister Agnes. As a child Ruth had been terrified of this woman to the point of having nightmares about her. Naturally she was horrified that Sister Agnes would come through to speak with her. As the reading progressed, Sister Agnes revealed that she had wanted to take this opportunity to tell Ruth the reason she had pushed her so hard at school was because she had seen her potential.

In the days when Ruth was in school, most girls were only expected to attend until leaving age then marry and have children. Ruth, however, had broken this mould. She had continued studying, became a nurse then ended up as a university lecturer. Sister Agnes explained to Ruth that they had not been brought together by accident. Through pushing her to achieve her potential, she had awoken Ruth to her vocation and steeled her ambition. This stood Ruth in good stead for the challenges that lay ahead of her as a pioneer in her chosen field.

Ruth sat there stunned and did not know how to take this information. When the spirit of her mother joined us, the reading continued in a much more relaxed manner.

Several weeks later we received a lengthy email from Ruth. She thanked us for connecting to her mother and also asked us to pass on her thanks to Sister Agnes. Ruth explained that she was lost for words at the time of the reading, but had now had a chance to reflect on the session and realised that Sister Agnes was right. Ruth had been given a whole new perspective. She also said that, thanks to her reading, she had taken great insight from Sister Agnes and was now able to see more clearly the reasons for the presence of various other people in her life and the repercussions they had.

We have all had the experience of meeting someone and just 'clicking' with them instantly—that feeling that we have known each other for years. Sometimes we meet someone and feel inexplicably drawn to them, just wanting to spend time with them although it doesn't seem to make sense. These are the feelings that arise when we meet members of our soul group because we recognise them on a spiritual level. Red Eagle explains it best. 'The soul recalls what the mind forgets,' he says. 'We are family after all.'

Soul groups exist for a variety of reasons and are not limited to family members and friends. A member of your soul group may be a teacher—as in Ruth's case—a boss, an acquaintance or even a stranger you meet only once. You can belong to more than one soul group at a time, just as you can belong to more than one social group in this world. For example, you may be a member of a church group and at the same time a member of your local swimming club. The same applies to soul groups. You may simultaneously belong to the soul group consisting of immediate friends and family you have planned to meet during your time on earth and also be a member of a larger more disparate soul group who are destined to leave this world during a military conflict. Naturally, you will not personally meet every other soldier who dies in the conflict while you are on earth, but you still have a soul connection through your common experience.

We have spoken before of the way great tragedy can unite people. A common cause rouses community spirit and selfish agendas can seem suddenly petty when people are confronted by their own mortality and vulnerability. In times of war, peace movements spring up. Natural disasters such as earthquakes and tsunamis provide us with a compassionate perspective and lead us to re-evaluate our priorities. Criminal acts ignite calls for justice. The experience of losing a loved one through terminal illness gives rise to charitable foundations being set up and promotes generosity. These reactions ripple outwards, impacting even those of us who have not been directly affected by sparking our sympathy.

The people we meet and the experiences we have shape our soul's growth, even if they seem insignificant. Our attitudes can be improved by others we encounter. Our friend Sue recently provided us with a great example of this. Sue was going to work and was in a particularly bad mood, dreading the long day ahead. On the way, she stopped to buy a cup of coffee. She told us that the bright smile and chirpy manner of the girl behind the counter cheered her instantly. As she left the cafe, Sue found herself smiling. 'Isn't it amazing,' she said, 'how a brief exchange with a complete stranger can improve your whole mind-set! It made me realise my grouchy demeanour was self-inflicted and unnecessary. I was so inspired that I chose to be happier too.'

Sue told us that being happier paid off immediately. 'I decided to smile more at work and the results have been great. Who would have thought that smiling could be so contagious! The office is a nicer place to be when you smile and others smile back.' This is the beauty of soul groups. A meeting with someone who seems to be a stranger in a cafe can actually be a spiritual interaction pre-planned before you were even born. These are the moments in which our souls grow.

Not all of us are born into the physical world to learn, how-ever. Some are born to teach. We recently had the privilege of meeting a young man in spirit by the name of Fred. Fred told us that he had been severely physically disabled during his lifetime and had died as a result of his body being bent in such a way that eventually there was too much pressure on his heart and lungs to survive. He described the frustration he felt at being unable to speak or move or express himself. He also spoke of the love and devotion of his grandparents who had cared for him. Fred told us that his grandfather's favourite saying was 'Don't take shortcuts.' Laughing, he said, 'Shortcuts? I couldn't take a shortcut if I wanted to! I couldn't even walk!'

Despite his physical disabilities, Fred's mind was perfectly intact. However, because people assumed it wasn't, he was able to observe both the best and the worst of human nature.

It would be all too easy to dismiss his existence as a wasted or pointless life. When confronted by the severely disabled, many people wonder what life lessons they are here to learn. Meeting Fred showed us that he was not here to learn . . . but to teach. His time on earth taught true compassion to those wise enough to learn it. How amazing that one disabled boy, without ever uttering a sentence, was able to instil in the hearts of those around him the very thing that all the great masters such as Jesus taught: compassion. And he never took a shortcut.

Even now from his place in the spirit world Fred continues to teach. He revealed to us that he holds no ill feeling towards his parents, who were unable to raise a severely disabled child and sent him to live with his grandparents. 'My parents did the best they could, I can see that,' he said. 'They just had too much on their plates to deal with me as well.' Fred extends the compassion he taught to others to his own parents and the beauty of his spirit shows us directly that the ability to forgive releases us from ongoing turmoil. Our hearts went out to Fred, and we gained valuable insight by meeting him.

As with every aspect of our lives, preplanning has gone into which members of our soul group we will encounter and why. The leeway of free will and the power to form our own opinions then come into play so that we can grow from making our own decisions and learn from our own mistakes. These things will affect what we take away from life's encounters and whether or not we learn from them. Of course, not everyone we meet in our lives is part of our soul family. It is nice to become acquainted with new people and broaden your horizons on any journey and the 'trip of a lifetime' is no different.

There are also members of our soul group who may not actually be living on earth at the same time as we are. Though they remain in the spirit world, they still form part of our network and can often play the role of helpers from the spiritual realms. Many people, including some who profess to having little belief in the afterlife, have told us stories about incidents that they find difficult to explain. For instance, Carol, a keen gardener in her sixties, was watering the garden and about to step backwards when she heard a voice in her head yelling, 'Don't step back!' Carol turned around and realised that had she done so, she would have stood on an upturned rake carelessly left there and injured herself.

Dennis, who we met socially, proclaimed to everyone who would listen that he had no belief in the afterlife, spirits or any such nonsense. But when we were alone with him, he could not resist taking the opportunity of telling us about an experience he had. Dennis was a nurse in a large hospital. One night when he was just beginning his shift, he heard a patient in one of the rooms getting out of bed to use the toilet. This particular patient was quite ill and had been in the ward for some time, and Dennis revealed that from the moment they met he felt they had a special bond. The patient had been repeatedly told he was not to get out of bed, but every night he would disobey the doctors' orders and get up at around nine o'clock to use the bathroom. Exasperated, Dennis rushed down the hall to stop him as he did every night. When he reached the room, however, it was empty and on returning to the nurse's station he found the daily notes telling him that the man had died that morning.

Dennis, the non-believer, told us that he thinks this man had come back just to get his attention and say goodbye. To this day he is bewildered by the episode, but says he believes in his heart it was because there was a bond between them.

It's obvious to us that these two men had a soul group connection. A reason, a season or a lifetime . . .

Whether they are living here on earth or in the spirit world, soul groups do share a bond. Over the years, we have become more and more aware that our main spirit guides are members of our soul group. They have accepted a big responsibility and a very difficult task in guiding us spiritually from their side of life's veil. Our mission as mediums is to connect people with their loved ones on the other side and prove that the bonds of love never die. Without our guides helping us, our task would be impossible.

To all the members of our soul group, and in particular to our spirit guides and helpers, we say thank you.

PART FIVE

End of the Line?

17

T.J.—The missing heartbeat of his family

'Even if you start going about it the wrong way over here, you still end up in the right place,' T.J. said to Ezio one night while he was working at his computer. T.J. had wanted us to once more connect him to his family before his sister Rhiannon moved interstate. Jokingly, he said he wouldn't reveal anything more about the afterlife until we acceded to his demands. 'I've already told you what it feels like to die. Now I'm ready to tell you what it's like over here, what it's like to be dead. But I want you to talk to my mother and sisters first. Please. I'd like you to talk with my dad too . . . but it might still be a while before he is ready to talk to you.'

'That'd be right. He was always trying to negotiate a deal,' Christine said when we called to arrange an appointment for another sitting. 'Even when he was a little boy he would always look for an angle. He called it "manoeuvring". Good to know he's still the same cheeky boy that Mummy loves.'

We met with Christine, Rhiannon and Teigen a few days later and T.J. easily made his presence known. All the work we had been doing together for this book had given him a practical insight into exactly what it took for his spirit to connect strongly to us. Communicating with a medium is not a natural occurrence for those in the spirit world. It doesn't hurt or adversely affect them in any way, it's just that they don't get to do it every day. As with anything in life, it takes practice.

With all the practice T.J. had in connecting to us during the last seven or eight months, he had become incredibly proficient at getting his message across. He had described the process of dying and leaving his body so beautifully that we were keen to hear what else he had to say about his new life in the spirit world. T.J.'s account of life as a spirit is particularly compelling because it was not long ago that he was one of us. He recounts his experience in real time; in the here and now. With the life he had just left behind still fresh in his mind, he is able to describe the process of dying and leaving his body in terms that we can all understand. T.J. is one of us, which makes his journey all the more relevant.

We thought he might reveal a little more about life on the other side during our session with his mother and sisters but T.J. was more interested in letting his family know that he was always nearby. Soon after everyone was settled, T.J. joined us. He was in a good mood, happy to be given another opportunity to get in touch with his family.

'Does my butt look big in this?' he said mischievously while showing us an image of his sister looking at her backside in the mirror. It wasn't quite what any of us expected. 'Looks like a new bikini to me.'

Rhiannon and Teigen looked perplexed. Neither of them had bought or tried on a new bikini in recent days—it was the middle of winter!

But T.J. would not be deterred. 'It *is* a new bikini!' he said and laughed, clearly amused at the confusion he had caused. He drew our attention to his mother by gently pushing our faces to turn and look at her. Christine said nothing.

'Did *you* buy the new bikini?' Michelle asked her.

Christine sighed, shuffled about in her seat then relented. 'No, I didn't . . . well, I did . . . but not for me. I bought the girls a new bikini each for Christmas. It was meant to be a surprise! I've hidden them in my wardrobe. The girls didn't know about the bikinis. Thanks T.J.!'

Despite her feigned annoyance, Christine was delighted that her son was able to show just how closely he still monitored her world. During our previous sessions, T.J. had learned that the people he loved took great comfort from such seemingly insignificant details because they proved he was right there with them. How else would he have known about the bikinis?

Our session continued for some time, with T.J. talking about many of his friends and family members, bringing up recent events to show as many people as he could that he was never far away and was watching over them too. We were both surprised and delighted at the concern he showed for the people he had left behind.

'They're my crew,' he said by way of explanation. 'We look out for one another.'

When his mother and sisters had left, T.J. came back into our reading room. 'Thank you for sitting with my mum and sisters. It means a lot to me that you do this for them,' he said politely. 'I'm ready to tell you what it's like over here.' Then he began to describe his experience of the spirit world.

•

'Over here, no one gets left behind. It really doesn't matter what you did to get over here. Whether you were sick or injured . . . or even killed. Sooner or later, we all end up in the same place.

'No one over here tells you what you should do or how you should live. You sort of just know that everything is okay. I haven't seen heaven or hell—not like you expect them to be anyway. But from the moment you arrive you get the feeling that you are part of something so much bigger. It's like everyone over here is in on a great big secret that people forget when you're down there. Up here we know the truth. Down there we don't.'

T.J.'s comments were intriguing to say the least. A truth that only those in the spirit world could access? We asked him to elaborate.

'It's about how we are all really part of one big family and that our earth families are like families within families. All you spiritual people talk about being connected to one another. I remember hearing it when I was alive and wondered exactly what it really meant. I sort of had an idea—that everyone is connected to everyone else. Even when I was down there I knew it was true. But on earth you only feel like you are connected to the people you love and that everyone else isn't part of your family. You don't think of your enemies as part of your family but they are. Not the family down there but the "bigger family" of spirits.

'After I died, Red Eagle called me aside and asked me if I knew who he was. I had never met him before but I said yes because I thought he felt familiar. He just laughed as if he knew I was faking it and he said not to worry, that in time I would remember everything. I was happy that he came to help me. He made me feel like everything was meant to be. He seemed to know Nanna and the rest of my family. I was really surprised that everyone seemed to be expecting me because I never expected to be dead at sixteen. Even now, I still can't find that memory in my soul that says it was meant to happen. But it doesn't feel like a mistake either. I guess at sixteen you just expect that you are going to live forever.

'I could sort of feel his heart beating inside my own chest—that's why I said that I knew him. I mean, I wouldn't have felt it if we weren't connected, right? I'm describing it like that because Mum and Dad would know exactly what I mean. For them, it's like their hearts skip a beat every now and then too. The one it skips used to belong to me. My heart used to beat in time with theirs and now it doesn't . . . well, at least they can't feel it anymore. That's why they feel so empty, because a part of them is missing. I just wish that I could make my world and theirs feel more connected. Maybe that way it wouldn't hurt them so much.'

T.J.'s description of his parents' loss was one of the most profoundly beautiful we have ever heard. He was a beat missing from the rhythm of his mother and father's hearts. We have never heard a parent's despair described so eloquently by anyone, let alone a teenage boy.

'No matter what happens from here on, I will always be Mum and Dad's son. I will always be Rhiannon and Teigen's little brother. We were family before we were born. That much I am sure of. I saw it in my mind. Like a picture showing me that we have always been family and always will be. As much as it hurts them to lose me, it was sort of planned that I would go on ahead of them. Just like Nanna and Uncle Ricky and Colin went up ahead of me. We go over first to make sure that the others are looked after when they get here. Dying isn't really about sad things, it's about being there for the people you love when they finish what they were down there doing and come back home.

'I'm starting to realise that even the people I didn't get along with are somehow part of my life. That's why I don't feel any real anger or hatred towards the guy that stabbed me. We shared our destiny. You can't really blame him for doing what he was born to do, can you? I mean, he still has to pay for it because that's his destiny too. Mine was to die and his is to pay for it. But, you know, I only died once. He has to pay for it on earth by going to jail and when he gets up here as well. That's when he will really cop it! Even if the courts do go light on him, which Mum and Dad are both freaking out about, he will still pay a heavy price in his soul.

'You can ignore your conscience when you're a person, but

you can't ignore it when you're a spirit. Your conscience is basically who you are over here. It is the voice of your soul. Remember that I told you before that I felt bad about the small bad stuff that I had done? When he gets here, there will be no judge or jury but he will feel a thousand times worse than I did, that's for sure. There's no escaping it. It's how we all move on. That horrible feeling inside is healed by the light inside you over time. That's the other part of the secret. People over here are not frightened to face up to what they did because they know that the light inside them will eventually take away the pain. Suffering doesn't last forever. You can be more honest with yourself if you know that the pain is going to be for only a short while. That honesty sends you to where you are meant to go next . . . to the next level.

'I'm really lucky. I was given the power to look back at my life before I was born, which is very cool. Apparently this is easier to do because I'm young. If I was older, like, say, 60 or 70, it would take longer to go back to my life before being born because living a lot of earth years clouds your sight. It comes back eventually . . . but it's lost for a while. It's different for everybody. That's the advantage of me being so young. By the time the old guys have cleared their earth memories and remember everything about where their soul came from, they have moved too deep into the spirit world and can't really get back close enough to earth to explain what it's like. The chance for them to tell everyone is gone.

'That's why I'm so in a hurry to get this stuff down on paper and have been pushing you two. I'm in a hurry!' T.J. said, laughing. 'It's almost time for me to move on too.'

18
The essence of soul growth

Our guides have always spoken of the soul's growth. Funnily, it is a concept that most people seem to understand instinctively, even if they can't define exactly what it means. For some reason, the idea of living so that our soul will grow and benefit from the experience just *feels* right. That is because it is part of our spiritual blueprint to continually expand our spiritual awareness. But what exactly is the soul? Is it the same thing as our spirit? How does it grow?

Red Eagle's definition is simultaneously elegant and simple. 'The soul is the part of you that is God,' he states plainly. 'The spirit is the vehicle that carries it from lifetime to lifetime. Both are indestructible. But only the soul is eternal.'

Michelle's spirit guide, Sarah, once told us a similar truth during a particularly stressful time in our lives. 'You are infinite,' she said. 'Keep it in perspective.' This advice helped us realise that the difficulty we were experiencing would soon pass and another patch of calm would prevail. It was the cycle of life, part of our soul growth. It was not personal. Just as we can experience growing pains in our physical bodies, sometimes the soul's expansion is accompanied by pains as well.

'Whatever we learn along life's journey comes back to us in times of need,' Red Eagle told us. 'Nothing you learn from lifetime to lifetime is ever wasted. We are born from life itself and therefore life is our parent, teacher, guardian and mentor. But life is not limited to just the existence you are having now. It is the sum of all the lives you live, including the ones yet to come. The person that you today believe yourself to be is largely a figment of your imagination. You are an eternal being. There is great power that comes from knowing that . . . and great wisdom.

'We move from lifetime to lifetime. Each one brings you a step nearer spiritual perfection. In an earthly sense, spiritual perfection may be described as reunion with God. Life on earth provides you with a unique opportunity to find your partnership with nature and your fellow man. The more connected you are to them, the more you are connected to our Creator. Sometimes it is easy. Other times it is a struggle. In one life, you may be someone who is born in an era of famine, unable to feed yourself or your family. In another, you may be a person who wields great influence or power, wanting for nothing. We learn equally from the bad times as we do from the good. Remember this, it will help you keep your own life in balance and harmony.'

We are fortunate to be spiritually guided by souls like Sarah and Red Eagle.

Over the years, our friends in the spirit world have revealed that the soul's journey and spiritual growth is the reason we are here. A soul grows by experiencing all that life on both sides of the veil has to offer. Physical life means getting to know the Creator by becoming more intimate with his creations. By sharing in the soul journey of other people, plants and animals, we become a part of them and they become a part of us. We learn things from their life and natural rhythms that we couldn't possibly learn from our life alone. Their existence makes our existence more complete. We are all just different pieces of one jigsaw puzzle.

In the spirit realms, we can choose the type of life we want by willing it into existence. Aside from being bodiless, this is the fundamental difference between the spirit and physical worlds. And while the afterlife does offer the soul growth that comes from reflection and remorse, selfrealisation is never really a titanic struggle like it can be here on earth. This life of privilege in the non-physical realm only enables us to grow and learn so much. In time, many of us become restless, bored with never having to strive for anything. Humans need the challenge of survival if they are truly to prosper. Given that there is not very much of the 'bad times' in the spirit world, it makes sense that we would have to go elsewhere to experience a variety of challenges. That 'elsewhere' is planet Earth.

There is a saying in spiritual circles—'As above, so below'—which implies that what takes place in the spirit world is replicated down here on earth. When we are in the spirit world, many of us choose to embark upon a new life adventure on the earth plane with all its pitfalls, challenges and obstacles. We do this because our soul yearns to become a more intimate part of something greater than itself. On earth, people also seek a greater connection to the world. They climb mountains even though they don't have to. They attempt mammoth sporting quests, cross burning desert plains, or venture deep beneath the ocean looking to discover something new about themselves or the planet they inhabit.

In most cases, there is no physical need to do any of it. We could exist just fine without climbing mountains, except that our soul just won't let it be. The soul demands new challenges, the discovery of new frontiers. These discoveries provide perspective to other facets of life which can be used to create a better world. We grow from the experience and others grow because we share those experiences with them. We don't all have to climb mountains to gain an insight into what it means to do so.

Whether they are essential or by choice, we learn from our challenges here too.

Red Eagle has often told us stories about his past life as a simple 'nature man', communing with plants and animals, living in harmony with the change of seasons, the rise and fall of the sun and moon. So we were very surprised one day when he said, 'I once lived a life as a merchant sailor.'

'Really?' we both asked him, not quite in disbelief but taken aback by the notion that such a gentle force of nature could have lived a lifetime as a rough and ready sea-faring man. Somehow, it didn't add up. He had always shown himself to us a tribal man who sang and drummed and prayed to the Great Spirit. Naturally, that is how we expected him to always be.

'It was during the nineteenth century,' he explained matter-of-factly. 'I was just a boy who had embarked upon a quest for manhood. I found sickness, disease and famine. The crew upon that ship were not honourable men. It was no place for a boy.'

When you know someone as well as we have come to know Red Eagle, it is a shock to discover that they had once been someone very different to the person you know and love today. You don't expect the quintessential native spirit guide to casually reveal that he was once a sailor. We have experienced something similar in our own lives where people that knew us in former life roles find it difficult to accept that we now work for the spirit world. Many old friends, former work colleagues and even family members have said that they find it difficult to believe we are mediums because they were not aware we had these abilities. Their point of view is understandable. There was never much need for mediumship in our former occupations as corporate services manager and speech pathologist.

Red Eagle was unperturbed by our obvious surprise at his latest revelation. He was teaching us to open our minds and expand our thinking. In one lifetime a person can be many things simultaneously—a parent, child, boss and sportsperson. So across lifetimes the possibilities are endless—a deeply spiritual nature man can be a sailor too!

Despite their lofty status in the grand scheme of things, our spirit guides never force us to accept what they teach if it doesn't feel right. If we are not ready to learn a new spiritual principle, they simply let it go until we are. They know that no matter how reluctant we might be to grasp some of life's mysteries, there is always time. Lifetimes, in fact.

It's as though all the past lives they have endured have given them an unlimited patience that the rest of us can't fathom. 'Fruit only ripens when it has spent long enough on the vine,' Red Eagle mused. 'People are the same. All nature is the same. If I were to share with you things that you are not ready to know, then my effort would be wasted and you would just be confused. I would rather that each of us spent our time more wisely.'

By revealing his past life as a sailor, Red Eagle had left the door of knowledge ajar, inviting us to peer inside if we should feel inclined. He was waiting to see if we understood the enormity of what he had just told us. Until today, he had always taught us about the mysteries of life from his perspective as a holy man of nature. Rarely did he feel the need to venture outside of that lifetime to impart wisdom and learning—although he had often invited other spirits into the fold to help broaden our understanding of life in both their world and ours.

Red Eagle was encouraging us to climb a mountain . . . take in a breathtaking new view. We were not blind to the opportunity. We are keen students after all and are always curious about what he might have learned from his past incarnations. Eager to hear more about one of his past-life experiences, we asked him what he'd learned from life as a sailor. Had he discovered new lands or had an island been named after him? Did he unearth jewels and diamonds and buried treasure hidden long ago by pirates?

Red Eagle smiled, then gave us an answer we were not expecting. 'I learned that the sea is no place for a boy to be among lawless men. I was twelve years old.'

His sombre words hit home with great force as the image of a young boy being mistreated by crusty old mariners seared itself into our minds. We looked at one another in amazement.

Red Eagle seemed unfazed by the trauma of his own horrible history. 'My life as a boy trapped with predators on the sea made me realise that children need to be protected. Until that lifetime, I had experienced no reason to think that any special treatment was warranted. All my previous childhoods had been quite idyllic.

'Natural communities are wonderful places for children to grow up. We were encouraged to explore our surroundings, find our own creativity and medicine. ['Medicine', to a nature person, is their own personal power or identity.] We were always an important part of our communities. When I embarked upon the sea-faring lifetime, I expected it to be fun and pleasurable like all the other childhoods I had known. It wasn't. Perhaps I should have taken greater care with my own spiritual itinerary!' he said, laughing to himself.

'Eventually, I threw myself overboard to escape the hostilities. So I have experienced drowning too,' he added, almost casually. 'When I jumped into the ocean, I remember feeling desperate and frightened but drowning seemed like a better option than remaining onboard.

'Upon crossing over, I was instantly welcomed and healed in the spirit world by family and well-wishers because I was a child who had suffered terrible trauma. It was like I had just awoken from a bad dream and discovered that I was safe at home. Never have I felt more loved, soothed or cared for than I did at that time. I recall that crossing-over episode being among the most uplifting soul encounters of my many lifetimes. It was so profound that it sparked my desire to learn all I could about the afterlife and share this with others. That is why I am a spirit guide today. A great deal of good came from that bad experience.'

There is no better way to discover the soul's reason for moving from one lifetime to another than to speak directly with a spirit guide. They are granted the privilege—as well as the difficulty and responsibility—of remembering all the lives they have lived. This gives them a greater perspective than the rest of us who can't access the past. They remember what the soul has been through to reach this point in time. Sarah's words echoed in our ears: *You are infinite—keep it in perspective!* Red Eagle had found perspective from a terrible lifetime. That perspective helped shape the spirit guide that he is today.

It was a lot to take in. The spirit guide who has so often told us that he was a nature man who hailed long ago from the place that is now known as Bolivia had also once been a merchant sailor. Just to make sure we were clear about what Red Eagle was teaching us, Ezio asked, 'So that particular lifetime was about learning that children need to be loved and protected?'

Red Eagle laughed softly, his compassion and patience melting away our uncertainty. 'No,' he said. 'I learned that unless I forgave those who hurt me, I would always be their victim.'

Once again, and with his usual eloquence, Red Eagle had summed it up for us. His lesson in forgiveness, not an easy one to learn and even less easy to have lived through, defines the struggle and the beauty that is the essence of soul growth.

19
Reincarnation— A round-trip ticket

As mediums, our job is to connect those still here on earth with their loved ones who have returned to the world of spirit. It is the cornerstone of our work and teaching. We are often asked how this is possible if there is such a thing as reincarnation. If a loved one has already reincarnated and returned to this world, how is it possible to communicate with their spirit?

Our guides are fond of saying that if you ask a spiritual question correctly, then the answer is self-evident. It is a reminder to keep things simple and not overcomplicate matters. By definition, reincarnation means leaving the spirit world and coming back to live in the physical world. So it is impossible to communicate with a spirit if they have already reincarnated. Not even a medium can communicate with someone who isn't there.

In earthly years the cycle of reincarnation is a long one. We have all heard expressions such as 'they live on in our hearts' or 'as long as we remember them they are not truly gone' when referring to those we have loved and lost. These sayings are never truer than where reincarnation is concerned. The reincarnation cycle for a soul in the spirit world begins when there is no one left on earth who has a living memory of them. As lovely as it may seem, it is unlikely that your father, for instance, will come back as your newborn son. Such a quick turnaround would create a risk that the child's memories of their previous life would leak through into this life, causing confusion as to their current role in the world.

So how can we be certain that reincarnation exists?

There have been many well-documented cases of people being born into this world who have remembered relatively recent past lives here. In 1990 a woman from Northamptonshire, England even met some of her children who, though now elderly, were still alive on earth. Jenny Cockell was able to give private details of her previous life including her name, where she lived, her children's names and where they were born. Undoubtedly the experience proved difficult for all concerned as an entire family grappled with the unlikely possibility that this apparent stranger was in fact a reborn relative and not someone with a psychological disorder. There is a heroic bent to such an aberration of nature. The pain and discomfort that this soul group went through demonstrated that reincarnation does happen. Cases such as this one are the exception that prove the rule.

Fortunately, such star-crossed lifetimes are exceptionally rare or this world would be a very confusing place. Imagine how mixed up we would be living one life while remembering a previous one. The old saying of not knowing whether you are Arthur or Martha might become literal!

As a rule, we don't remember previous lives while we are here. That is why it is best that reincarnation does not happen until there is no one left on earth with any memory of the person we once were. It saves confusion and heartache such as in the story above.

Still, there is something quite romantic and noble about the concept of meeting up with beloved family members in a new lifetime and era. Time and time again, we have been asked whether somebody's new baby could be a reincarnation of, for example, their grandmother. Given the parents and others can still vividly remember their grandmother, this is highly unlikely. It is not unusual for the parent asking us the question to be visibly upset by our response. Often, they were willing it to be true. One young mother told us that she loved her child so much more because it felt like she was not only loving her newborn baby, but that she was also loving her dear departed grandmother whom she adored. 'Elise is so much like Nanna,' she pleaded. 'You really don't think that this is her?'

There are two very good reasons why a new child in a family may strongly resemble or have traits and characteristics of a deceased relative. The first and most obvious is genetic— inherited physical features or personality traits which run in the family and give the new little one a striking resemblance

to their ancestor. Long-term studies of this phenomenon indi-
cate that familial characteristics are nature's way of ensuring
that parents accept their offspring and feel a natural urge to
protect them. While this is physiologically true, in spiritual
terms it's also about soul family. There are certain qualities
that make members of the same soul family more recognisable
to one another.

The second reason is far more intriguing. Because they
have not been in the physical world for very long, babies
and young children are very open to the spirit world from
where they've recently come. A young child is still very much
attuned to the vibration of the non-physical realms, which
means they can more easily perceive the presence of a spirit
than an adult can. It is quite common for babies and young
children to see their loved ones in spirit. As a consequence,
they may pick up mannerisms or copy certain unique expressions from spirits that make their parents think that they are
the reincarnation of a deceased loved one.

Stephanie's son Jason is a perfect example of this. Stephanie's brother John died as the result of a car accident when
he was just sixteen. Her son Jason was born almost ten years
later. From about the age of eighteen months when Jason was
beginning to talk, he would often go quiet during play, stare
at one spot, point and then start laughing at what seemed
like nothing. When his language developed a little more, he
would accompany his pointing and giggling by saying 'man'.
Stephanie kept asking Jason who the man was but he just
repeated the word 'man'. Stephanie and her family are quite
religious and she was a little concerned with Jason's behaviour

but decided it was best to keep it to herself and hope that he would soon grow out of it.

Time went on and one day, when Jason was around three years old, Stephanie took him to visit his grandparents. They decided to look through some old photo albums and when he saw a picture of Stephanie's brother John, Jason piped up excitedly: 'Mummy, the man! The man—there!'

'I was so shocked,' recalled Stephanie. 'I couldn't believe it! Jason had been seeing my brother who died ten years before he was even born. It took me a while to come to grips with it, but I like to believe that John is up in heaven watching over my boy and protecting him. I'm not as surprised now as I was initially—the older Jason gets, the more I see a resemblance to John. They share the same genes, the same mannerisms. They would have gotten on really well.'

Episodes like the one Stephanie's family experienced demonstrate the way in which children can be influenced by their relatives in the spirit world. Given that the time between our trips to earth is long, possibly one hundred years or more, it is improbable that new family members are the reincarnation of deceased loved ones.

When we return to spirit our lives do not end and our journey continues. Our time in the spirit world is used in many ways. We need to contemplate and absorb the experiences of the life just lived and receive any healing we may require. Naturally, we reconnect with those with whom we shared our recent lifetime and returned to spirit before us. We meet up with our soul group to exchange ideas to help us understand our experiences more profoundly—in the afterlife, what each spirit has learned is shared with everyone and more pieces of life's jigsaw puzzle fall into place.

So it makes sense that we need a break between incarnations. Often, after a hectic trip spent sightseeing and experiencing new things, rushing from place to place so you don't miss anything, you return home feeling as though you need some time to rest and recover. So it is with our journey to the earth plane. You need a 'holiday after your holiday'.

Once rested, we may choose to work in the spirit world as a protector for our earthly family or to perform some other service, such as Marcus does in helping mediums (see Chapter 10) or Shelley who has chosen to work with children (see Chapter 15). Or we may decide if and when we will reincarnate. If we are going to return to earth, we must once again plan our new itineraries. What country will we live in, what religion will we follow? Which members of our soul family will travel with us into a new life? Perhaps we will include the things we didn't see or do last time when planning the itinerary for our next trip. There are so many considerations.

Personally, we know that reincarnation takes place because we have been given glimpses into some past lives of our own—including ones we have shared together. When we first met in this lifetime, it was as if a portal into the past had opened before us and each of us was flooded with memories of lives that we had shared together. We both had an acute sense that we were already husband and wife well before we were married. When we finally reunited in this life, we simply picked up where we had left off. This past-life flashback occurred with the assistance of our guides and only took place because it was absolutely necessary for our learning and teaching. The spirit world wanted to make sure that we remembered we were meant to be together—despite the difficulties that such a reunion entailed. We have been very privileged to have this authentic snapshot of our own past lives but it is not something that should be taken lightly.

Our friend and experienced journalist Barry Eaton retraced his own past life in his 2011 book *Afterlife*. Working with a qualified and reputable practitioner, Barry was able to chart his own past-life footsteps back to the Somme during World War I. But Barry did more than simply regress through his own subconscious mind. He physically jumped on an aeroplane and ventured overseas to test the authenticity of his regression. In *Afterlife*, he recounts his own history as an independent third party, watching his own past life with curiosity and surprise as one might watch a movie. Visiting the places where he had once fought and died helped Barry put many of the issues in his current life into a new perspective. What he learned from the past helped him in the present. People such as Barry are given a rare and detailed look at their past life so they can share it with others. It's another example of an exception that proves the rule. It happens so others can learn from it, without having to endure the discomfort of it for themselves.

Trying to access past lives during our time on earth can be very helpful if there is a genuine need for it and if the practitioner you work with is authentic and trustworthy. A properly conducted past-life regression can unlock and release many subtle fears and ingrained beliefs that might be affecting your life today. However, if handled incorrectly or performed for the wrong reasons, it can also be dangerous and detrimental. Mere curiosity is not a valid reason for having a past-life regression. The true purpose of a past-life regression is for healing and moving beyond the limitations we may have experienced in the past so that we can get on with a more worthwhile future.

If we were all meant to remember our past lives in the present world, then we would. That we don't remember them in detail is telling. The experiences we have had in other lifetimes undoubtedly impact upon us on a soul level. We carry that experience and the knowledge it brings with us from lifetime to lifetime. In the present day, much of this experience rises to the surface of our consciousness as an innate knowing or intuition. Quite literally, the knowing that comes from past lives—or life between lives—is your natural sixth sense.

This is, of course, all taken into account when we plan our spiritual itineraries. But imagine the conflict and anguish which would be unleashed if, for example, in this life you are a loving, gentle husband and father who works as a doctor because your core beliefs are humanitarian and you suddenly discover that in a past life you were a cruel and merciless executioner who loved torturing and killing people? The mental and emotional fallout from this would be crippling. Such a contrast in lifetimes is not easily reconciled and can derail what you came here to do.

With past-life regression being trendy and seeming like a fun thing to do, it is worth taking a few moments to point out some inherent dangers. An obvious one is that a practitioner doesn't need any qualification to be a past-life regression therapist. The other is that there is no way of proving that what you are told is true. Many people who delve into past lives for the thrill factor expect to be told that they were royalty or lived some other rich and glamorous existence. In reality, most of us in this life are ordinary people—and so we have been previously. But who wants to be told they were a dirt poor potato farmer who struggled all their lives just to feed their family?

It brings to mind an old movie we once watched where some spiritual new-age types were complaining about a colleague behind her back. 'My goodness,' the first woman said about their colleague, 'she thinks that she was Cleopatra in a past life!'

'That's impossible,' the second woman replied. 'How could she be? *I* was Cleopatra in a past life!'

Wishful thinking aside, the other danger of past-life exploration is using it as a crutch or blaming past-life issues for problems in our current lives. If you have difficulties in the here and now, then, in most cases, this is the place to acknowledge them and try to address them. Say, for example, you have difficulty in romantic relationships. Rather than deciding it must be because you were a heartbreaker and a cad in a past life, you need to examine your behaviour and patterns in this life for a way to resolve your issues. Life requires that we take personal responsibility for our own actions. Using real or imagined past-life transgressions as an excuse for shortfalls in this life is pointless. It simply allows us to give ourselves permission to give up rather than work on a solution.

There are, of course, times when past-life regression has genuinely helped people overcome problems in this life. There was the case of Mandy, a school teacher, who at around 30 years of age suddenly developed an extreme terror of heights. She could not climb stairs or even a stepladder and the problem became debilitating. With the help of an experienced and trustworthy therapist Mandy discovered that in a past life she had been killed in a fall at the age of 30. Once this was brought to light and dealt with through ongoing therapy and counselling, she was able to overcome her fear and resume a normal life.

Fears and phobias, especially those that develop suddenly and seemingly out of nowhere, are among the rare cases when this kind of regression can be of assistance. This course of action is only recommended when all other obvious explanations have been ruled out. But, remember, if you choose to investigate past lives without good cause, there is a risk that you will uncover or relive events that are traumatic and may adversely affect your life.

Our spirit guides are a rich source of knowledge on past lives and reincarnation. Many people who begin working with spirit become confused because, as they get to know their guide through the practice of meditation and dedication, they may see them in different ways. Spirit guides are highly evolved beings and have generally lived many, many lifetimes on the earth plane. Red Eagle chuckles as he tells us that he has experienced death so many different ways during his many lifetimes: 'I have been stabbed, speared, burned and died from natural causes. And I can assure you—death is a myth!' Unlike the rest of us, spirit guides are able to access their past-life experience at will so that they can share the knowledge they have accumulated along the way. As a result they have a wealth of experience to draw upon when helping us.

In addition, spirit guides are able to present different aspects of themselves to us based on what we need at the time. Although Red Eagle describes himself as a nature man from the area now known as Bolivia, he recently enthralled us with tales of two of his other lifetimes—one as a merchant sailor, the other as a Christian missionary of sorts. Sarah, Michelle's spirit guide, who normally appears as a medieval priestess, has presented herself once or twice as an elderly Native American medicine woman—calling upon aspects of another lifetime she has lived to teach and guide her student. The cultural image that a spirit guide uses when showing themselves to their medium is a reflection of the type of learning or energy that the medium needs at that time.

After one of our public readings, a lady approached us to say that she had really enjoyed the evening, not just for the messages from spirit but because she had learned so much from watching us work. 'And, oh boy,' she said seriously, 'when you die and are spirit guides, I bet that you're going to be really strict on the mediums you work with!'

We both thought this was hilarious and Ezio told her so. 'Us? Spirit Guides?' He laughed. 'We still have way too much to learn before we can become spirit guides.' Our round-trip ticket has many unused frequent flyer miles on it yet!

20
The travel bug bites!

Life before life, life after life and reincarnation—most people have an instinctive sense that there has to be more than just this earthly existence.

In our hearts, we know that we are part of something bigger than ourselves. We don't need to be told, we can feel it. Many people have described this feeling as a yearning or a sense that something is missing. To try and quell those feelings and fill the void, some explore different religions, faiths and mystical practices. Others are fortunate enough to have personal experiences or beliefs that bring them an inner peace. That is really the key—your own infinite soul with its wealth of experience and lifetimes of learning really does contain the answers you seek.

We choose to come to earth and live within a certain religion, lifestyle and culture for the experience they will give us. Unfortunately, because we don't have access to this pre-life information while we are here, life can seem frustrating, unfair and at times just downright disappointing. But life also promises an experience that is at times both rewarding and joyful. It is a heady mixture that our souls find irresistible. Like a honey bee drawn to the sweetest smelling flower in the garden, we just can't keep away.

Each lifetime is an event in itself. When it is over and we return to the spirit world, we are given the time needed to make our peace with what has just transpired and absorb what we have learned into our soul during our life review process (see Chapter 22). The life review is the opportunity each spirit has to examine the life they have just lived. This is how our soul grows from the experience we have just had. When this process is complete, we may well choose to return at some stage in the future. But why does the travel bug bite so often? What lure of the physical world could make us want to leave the relative comfort of the spirit realm and re-enter physical life again and again?

As always, our spirit guides have the answers. A great deal can be learned from those in the spirit world through a process called 'trance mediumship'. This rather scary-sounding name simply means that the medium enters a relaxed state of altered consciousness and allows the spirit guides to speak through them. Trance mediumship is a real gift as it provides an opportunity to converse directly with a spirit who is still actively living and working in the spirit realms. We consider it to be a sacred practice and part of our own learning experience. We never enter into it lightly, or for any other reason than to learn from those residing in higher spiritual realms. Sometimes during these sessions, our students are invited to converse directly with our guides and spirit helpers, such as Marcus, Edgar the delightful bush poet and Red Eagle, to ask questions regarding their development as mediums or to discuss larger philosophical concerns they may have.

Our spirit helper Marcus once joked that communicating through Ezio via trance mediumship was like having another earthly experience, without having to suffer all the inconvenience that goes with it. 'It's like I am reborn and able to have my say once more,' he declared boldly. 'Only this way, I don't have to endure all those helpless years as a baby. It's far more practical to speak with you in this manner. Directly and to the point. By communicating through an entranced medium, I get to speak freely on any number of topics like only a spirit can, unbound by trivialities such as social convention. Don't you agree?'

It is difficult not to. It is far quicker to communicate through an entranced medium than it is to be reborn so that you can share what you know!

It is always interesting to watch people's reactions to these sessions. Some, stunned into silence, will sit quietly and take it all in. Others, sensing a rare and beautiful opportunity to learn, grab the chance to talk directly with a spirit who can give them a personal insight into the mysteries of life and death. Occasionally, there are those who want to test the spirits to make sure that they are not being conned. During a session with Red Eagle, a woman tried to trip him up with what she believed to be a tricky question regarding the lack of spirituality in this world. Red Eagle has a simple outlook when it comes to the mystery of life. He says that we are related as children of the Great Spirit so we should find ways of loving each other no matter what.

'If what you say is true, Red Eagle, and we are all spiritual beings from the same source and all connected, why are there so many evil and nasty people in this world? Why are people materialistic and selfish?' the woman asked and sat back smugly waiting for an explanation.

With his usual calm dignity and grace, Red Eagle answered her question with one of his own. 'I see you lament your life circumstance as often unfair,' he said, 'and you question the motives of others. I would ask you this. The people of India are known to have a very strong spirituality. It is evident throughout their culture. What do you think a poor starving Indian child who lives on the street is thinking about?'

The woman didn't pause to think about it. 'Well, karma, obviously!' she replied.

'No,' said Red Eagle. 'That child is not thinking about his karma. He is thinking only about where his next grain of rice is coming from and how to get it.'

It was enough to make us wonder why someone would choose to live a life where it is a battle just to keep from starving when there are far better options. What happens as a consequence of that life? This is where the travel bug can truly start to bite.

That starving child, like each and every one of us, is a spirit connected to all that is. Although poor and seemingly of little consequence, he is very much still part of the big picture.

The indelible impression such a difficult life would undoubtedly leave on his soul must have an impact. Eventually this starving child dies and returns to the spirit world. It is the completion of a cycle of life, the end of another experience.

Logically, the most obvious reason for him to reincarnate may be simply for the chance at living an easier or longer life on earth next time around. With a little luck and some foresight in planning, he will have a better opportunity to be happy and healthy because he is not solely focused on the challenge of surviving. His next life might be a reward or recognition for what he has previously endured. The true beauty that comes from the blending of that previous harsh existence and a new life can shine in many ways.

Perhaps with a new and carefully planned spiritual itinerary that child may reincarnate and become a great philanthropist with the power, resources and, most importantly, the desire to help the poor and starving of the world. His own past-life experience results in a natural compassion and empathy for those who suffer, driving him to help others less fortunate than himself. On the surface, exactly what motivates him may be a mystery both to himself and to those around him, but his dedication and selflessness are there for all to see. His inspiration to help the poor comes from the deepest level—the level of the soul. It is a direct result of his past-life lessons.

Living this new life impacts not only upon those he helps through his generosity and goodwill, but also affects others who are inspired by his kindness. He is a role model who leads by example. Word of the remarkably charitable nature of this one person ripples out into the wider community and inspires others to be better people. In turn, they are inspired to give of themselves as well. We have all seen examples of this in people such as Mother Teresa and Doctor Fred Hollows who both worked relentlessly to help the poor. Long after they return to the spirit world, the legacy of their work remains intact and continues to inspire others.

Sometimes, however, even the best laid plans go awry. A life of privilege, even with the best pre-planned intentions, is not without its pitfalls. Remember our old friend 'free will'? It may happen that, once here in the physical world, our champion becomes distracted by worldly concerns and puts other things ahead of helping those in need. It would be unfair to judge him harshly for that—he is probably entitled to a life of comfort given his previous difficulties. But what happens when it's all over and he returns to the spirit world to find that somewhere along the way he missed doing what he set out to do? You guessed it, the wider perspective gained by this knowledge would more than likely cause that travel bug to bite yet again.

Each time we return to earth, we bring with us the many gifts that we accumulated over all our previous lifetimes. The more lifetimes we've had, the wiser we are—or should be. Nothing we ever do from lifetime to lifetime is wasted. In fact, our strengths as well as our weaknesses are considered and used each time we embark on a new trip to earth, a new life. There are numerous accounts of people having skills that seemingly arise out of nowhere. For example, child prodigies who arrive here on earth remarkably gifted and talented at music or art have undoubtedly brought skills that they acquired in a previous life. They more or less pick up where they left off. That is not to say that effort and hard work was not required for them to reach that level of ability, but they had a running start because of what they had already learned in previous lifetimes. Quite often, these people are referred to as old souls, which means that they appear to have an ageless wisdom.

In the physical world with all its conflicting priorities, we lack the perspective gained from the broader overview so freely available in the spirit world. Our helicopter view is grounded. All we can see is what is right in front of us. We forget that we are infinite beings and that death is an illusion. We see death as the end of the line when really it is not. Death is a transition, the energetic current through which the spirit passes from world to world. We are not gone when we die, we have just left the physical world behind for a while and re-entered the spirit world. Once there, with renewed perspective and enthusiasm, we begin to plan our future adventures because we know that there is so much more out there that we haven't yet experienced.

Our reasons for returning time and time again are many and varied. It all depends on what our soul needs to grow. Each and every one of us who has chosen to be on earth has a role to play. Last time around, you may have been an unfortunate child, learning all the lessons that a child of such circumstance would learn. Next time, you may be a doctor, or a judge, or a housewife. There is no order of merit, each role is equally important. We can't all be rich or famous or incredibly talented. What we can be is grateful for our own place in the grand scheme of things. If we focus on living our lives day by day, being the best person we can be, we will make a difference to the world. If we focus on less noble characteristics, such as jealousy and envying the lives of others, we may well miss out on our own joys and achievements.

However, it is not only those who live in the physical world that influence it. Many people in the spirit realms play a significant role in shaping life on this planet. There are those such as spirit guides and helpers who choose to remain in the spirit world and still have a hand in the lives of those in the physical world, such as by helping people connect with their loved ones who have crossed over.

And yet it would seem that our spirit guides and helpers have been bitten by the travel bug too. With all the lifetimes of learning behind them, one could be excused for thinking they had earned the right to sit back in heaven and watch the world go by. But a soul only reaches the lofty status of spirit guide because they have a great and abiding love for the world and everything in it. They know that the more of us that awaken to the understanding that we are a unique and special part of creation, the better the world will be.

We asked Michelle's guide Sarah if she could explain to us what drives the need to come back time and again. This is how she described it:

'Imagine your soul appearing as a gentle whirlwind, a softly swirling spiral of moving air. When we start out we are like the very bottom point of that whirlwind, at the place where it touches the ground. With each successive lifetime we live, our soul grows and expands, naturally both widening the spiral and stretching it further skyward. This is a gentle and methodical ongoing process. The experiences of each life lived result in the expansion of our soul and allow us to stretch a little more each time. Your soul grows by embracing the lessons of compassion, forgiveness and love learned along the way.

'Eventually, with enough time and experience, the spiral becomes so high and so very wide that it is impossible to distinguish from the sky around it, the very air that it was born of in the first place. It blends in perfectly with its surroundings. So it is with your spirit—you eventually complete the cycle and once again return to the place where you started—the place of being truly connected with all that is.

'That, in essence, is why we keep coming back. Like the gently swirling whirlwind we must keep moving. Our destiny is to learn and grow and to contribute, and we continue to do so until we return to and blend joyfully with the very source of life.'

PART SIX

The Journey Never Ends

21

T.J. remembers

'It is almost a year since I died,' T.J. told us. 'It feels longer. I think that I died young so I could teach people not to be afraid to live. If I have a legacy, then that's it. Don't be afraid to be yourself because life is going to happen to you anyway.'

T.J. was in a more reflective mood than usual, speaking so quietly that he was barely audible above the din of cockatoos as they sought evening roost in the bushland outside our home. It was late October, almost twelve months since he had left this world and journeyed to the other side. On this day, there was definitely something different about his spiritual vibration. It was still vital and strong but there was a floaty feeling to his spirit that had not been there before. We soon discovered that this would be the last time the gates of spiritual communication between his world and ours would be so fully open. T.J. was taking the next step in his journey, his young soul readying to travel forward to the next phase of his life in spirit.

'It's time for me to move on,' he said softly. 'I'm ready now. After this, you will still be able to communicate with me when my family comes to see you but only in the same way that you communicate with other spirits. It won't be like it is now. Red Eagle tells me that our work together is done. I've been able to get through to you so clearly because he has let me communicate on his own personal wavelength. I've really enjoyed it. I hope you have too.'

The relationship between a medium and their spirit guide is an intensely personal one that develops over many lifetimes. It is the classic master and pupil story where the fumbling young student finds their way to their teacher, who is able to open the student's heart so they may grasp their destiny. The bond we share with our guides is a unique and special one but Red Eagle has always maintained that Ezio is not his only student. He has told us many times that he guides and assists a number of other mediums around the world with their spiritual development and understanding. Now T.J. was one of his students too. We knew he was in good hands.

Communication with our spirit guides is clearer than normal spirit contact because we are attuned to their 'frequency' in a way that is not generally possible with other spirits. Guides are like the voice of our conscience, like Jiminy Cricket in the Disney movie *Pinocchio*.

When T.J. said he communicated with us on Red Eagle's wavelength, he meant that he had been able to transmit his messages through a stream of consciousness that enabled his thoughts to flow directly into our minds. It is similar to using a high speed internet connection to receive data quickly and accurately to your computer. That flow was about to slow as T.J. readied for the next stage of life in the spirit world.

Next, T.J. began to speak of his life review—the process where we do a debrief of our lives once we are settled into the spirit world.

'I have been shown my life in a way that I never saw it before,' T.J. said. 'It's a bit freaky. I could see how my actions affected others, how the things I did or didn't do changed the world I lived in. It's like the entire universe is a living thing that is changed, hurt or improved by the actions and interactions of everyone and everything. Red Eagle said that each one of us is a cell in the body of the world. That's why his people called the world 'Mother'. That is also why we need to take responsibility for our actions. Whatever we do—or don't do—we affect things, so we need to be aware of affecting things in a positive way. I think I always knew that somehow, felt it inside me when I was alive. But I never really understood how it all worked.

'Having a life review is pretty cool. I mean, how many kids my age do you know who get the chance to see their own life flash before their eyes and then get to tell everyone about it?' He laughed cheekily, lightening up significantly from the more subdued mood he first presented when we sat at our computer to type his message. 'I'm going to miss being able to do this . . . I still have a lot to say!'

As much as T.J. is now part of the spirit world, the bond of love he shares with his family and his crew remains as strong as ever. He is acutely aware of what they are feeling and though he has his own point of view regarding the spiritual big picture, he empathises with them, understands their feelings and continues to support them with his love.

As we prepare to go to print, T.J.'s family have yet to face the horror of the upcoming trial of his accused killer. His hope is that being able to share his story through us will go some way to comforting those he loves and others like them who have lost loved ones suddenly or in tragic circumstances.

'I guess the first thing I should talk about is my stabbing.' T.J. continued. 'My death still hangs over everyone that knew and loved me. It is still a big deal to all of them and will be until the trial and all the appeals are finally dealt with—maybe longer. But, you know, over here they gave me a chance to look back over my life and see the things that were really important—and guess what? *Dying wasn't even in the top three!* Down there, we talked about earning respect and being true to yourself and your family and friends. But it all comes down to love . . . about not being afraid to love your friends, your family, your life.

'You want to know what the top three most important things were in my life? I'll tell you. First, there was my family—Mum, Dad, Rhiannon and Teigen. Not just as individuals, but all together as a group. They are at the top of my list. I was shown that we had all agreed to have a life down there together. We were the centre of our own universe. I just hope that they find strength in one another and that my death doesn't tear them apart, because it's not the end. We are meant to be together again and will be.

'The second thing is that you are given a certain amount of time down there and you never know when that time is up. So make the most of it! That's definitely number two—make the most of your life because feeling and appreciating all the good things that the world has to offer is just the best! It might seem like the time I spent down there was short . . . but for what my spirit needed, what my soul needed, it was perfect. Time is not about watching a clock ticking, it is a gift to us and one that we should use to live! Time is just a package, all gift-wrapped . . . but it's what you do with that package that really counts.

'The third thing is my crew. You know what is really surprising? When you're dead, you realise that the whole world is your crew! Even the bad guys you meet, they are part of your life and destiny so they are part of your crew too. I saw it all in my life review. I could see that everyone had a role to play, just like a football team. There are people who will be the stars and others who plug away and do the hard yards. Some people stand out more than others—but everyone is equally important.

'My life review was like dreaming while I was awake. I saw my life in my mind like you do in a dream, but knew that I was just watching it, not actually living it. The closest thing I could describe it to is maybe like being hypnotised.

'And they show you the strangest things too. When I was fighting off the guy with the knife, I could tell that he was thinking, "Just run away, you stupid jerk." He didn't want to kill me but he was too worried about what his mates would think to back down. The fool wanted to show how tough he was, that he was a man. He wanted me to run away so he didn't have to go through with cutting me! That was never going to happen. I always thought I had the situation under control. Obviously I didn't. He was acting tough in front of the other guys and I was trying to show them that I wasn't scared. How stupid is that? Suddenly I realised how ridiculous it was to care so much about what other people thought of me, especially since they weren't my family. Dad, Mum, Rhiannon and Teigen, they are the ones I should have worried about. They were the last thing I thought of when I crossed over and the first thing I remembered about my life when I got over here. In my review, I felt all their pain and sadness at losing me. I also felt how sad they had been in the past when they lost other loved ones. Feeling those things has made me a better person.

'But getting back to the fight that ended my life, during my review I could see that we both had a choice. He could have walked away, made a decision that would have changed the whole drama, and so could I—but we didn't. His ego drove him to killing me and my pride stopped me from walking away. I don't know whether it would have made a difference to how long I lived. But—and I don't want to upset anyone—I doubt it would have. I'm pretty sure it was my time to go, one way or another. I did what I had to do down there, learned about loving people with all my heart. That's enough, really.

'I was surprised that there was nothing random about my life. It was no mistake that I was born into Mum and Dad's lives. It was all pre-planned. Even before I was born, there was something inside of them that knew I was coming. They didn't know it consciously but they knew it in their souls.

Deep down, maybe my family had a clue that I was only going to be in the world for a short time. I'm pretty sure that my sisters did. They always fussed over me, making sure I was looked after. They acted more like little mothers than sisters! Even as I got older and basically conned them to do everything for me, they always threatened that they were going to stop. "This is the last time, Toddy!" they would say. But it never was . . . I was so cute, they just couldn't help themselves!

'It's funny the things that stand out in my mind. Once, in science, the teacher made us put this gunk in a Petri dish. It was some sort of jelly. Then we dropped something into it—I don't remember what exactly—but it started growing almost instantly. The teacher called them organisms. It's the closest thing I can think of to describe how life is connected. Everything is attached to something else that can make it grow or die. I don't remember all the details of that experiment—and at the time I didn't really pay that much attention—but I always remembered what it looked like. During my life review it helped me understand how we are all connected. We are all organisms that live as part of each other.

'You do feel differently about things when you're dead. Maybe that's one of the reasons you go through a life review. It's hard to be angry or hold a grudge when you realise that we are all just part of a big drama down there and that death is not really the end. Up here, you don't seem to be so emotionally invested anymore so you look at things more plainly. Here, you learn pretty quickly to just live for love. You learn to forgive too. That's important.'

Christine told us that not long before he died, T.J. was

offered an opportunity to study journalism. 'He always had such a good way of expressing himself,' she said. 'He just had a natural way with words.'

We have to agree. The way T.J. has been able to describe, in a way we can all understand, his transition into the spirit world and his experiences there so far has been wonderful.

'Your boy may not have been a journalist while he was here,' Ezio told her, 'but he is definitely a journalist now, reporting from the afterlife!' Part of his itinerary? We think so. Nothing is ever wasted!

T.J.'s final earthly mission has been to generously share with those of us still here what he has learned through living and dying and continuing his journey in the spirit world. Love one another. Don't be afraid to live. Use your time wisely and make choices so your impact on the world is a positive one. Nothing is a mistake or happens randomly. Even this book—if you are reading it, you were meant to. Just as we were meant to meet Christine so that when it was his time to go, T.J. would still have a voice.

T.J.'s final words?

'I want you to tell my family that it's alright for them to live. I want them to grab life with both hands and to live it strong! They shouldn't hold back because I'm not there . . . that would be a huge waste. Tell them to live! They have to start thinking about their own lives otherwise they will always be victims of my death too. I don't want that. They know me and know I wouldn't stand for it if I was still there. Tell them to remember that the time we spent together was a gift. Tell them that I am proud to call them family.'

22
Life review— The journey revisited

The priest stood in the far back corner of the room. The only indication that he was a man of the cloth was the small gold crucifix pinned to his lapel that caught and reflected the overhead lights as he shuffled about. He didn't appear comfortable standing in a room full of people hoping to receive a message from their loved ones in the spirit world. The room was quite small and the priest's efforts to blend into the background only made him stand out more.

During the evening, a warm and loving spirit calling himself Ron drew our attention to the priest standing in the shadows of the auditorium. 'He had an accident,' Ron told us. 'It has changed his entire outlook.'

Many religions have long protested the dangers of spiritual mediumship, but our guides have taught us to respect all religions so we're careful about what we say to whom. But Ron was insistent and, ultimately, our work as mediums is to pass on messages from spirit, so that's what we did.

To our amazement, the priest, who later told us his name was Father Michael, appeared to genuinely welcome the message we conveyed. Naturally, we were relieved. We soon discovered Ron was his father who had died of lung cancer a number of years earlier. The love Ron had for his son was among the strongest we have ever felt.

'Tell him I was there when he had the accident and I know what happened,' Ron said. 'He saw me! I don't want him to deny it anymore.'

We have all heard that at the moment of impending death someone who has a narrow escape sees their life flash before their eyes. This is what happened to Father Michael when his car careened off the road late one evening and crashed into a tree. But while the ambulance officers worked feverishly to save him, his spirit was having an entirely different experience elsewhere . . .

'He is right,' Father Michael acknowledged solemnly when we sat down for a chat with him after the show. 'I did see him while I was out there. My dad was a very strict Irish Catholic who never deviated from his religious faith. When he died, I felt a great sorrow that I carry with me even today. While I was unconscious, I didn't see tunnels or bright lights, although I certainly felt like I was being pulled along by some unseen force. I didn't see any evidence of heaven or hell . . . I only saw my dad.

'He was standing right there in front of me, as clear as day.

He told me that I wouldn't be staying and joked that I was on a temporary visa so I shouldn't make myself too comfortable. He was always a bit of a mad Irishman.'

Father Michael went on to reveal that while in this altered state, he experienced a form of debriefing of his life so far: 'My father told me that I was to make sure I took in all the beauty of God's world, and not to just rest on my laurels and accept that the teachings of my faith were the only ones I should adhere to. He said that there was truth in all of it and that I should live the rest of my life with my eyes wide open. That's a pretty hard thing for a priest to accept. It's one of the things that brought me to see you.

'When I had recovered, I spoke to some other priests about what had happened. To a man, they all said that it wasn't really my dad and that it was probably an agent of Satan. Every one of them! They all toed the company line. Then I realised that I had been doing the same thing. Before the accident I was just so certain . . . I had dedicated myself to a life of service to a single religion and forgot to pay attention to everything else.'

'Have you ever heard of a life review?' Michelle asked him.

The priest shook his head. 'No . . . but I think I understand the concept. It's like being called to account?'

'Well, sort of,' Michelle replied. 'Most of us have heard of the concept that when we die and reach the spirit world we go through a "life review" process. This is sometimes described as being seated on a grand throne in a room like a theatre and watching our lives unfold before us on the big screen. We are shown what we did right and more importantly what we did wrong during our lifetime and feel appropriate remorse for those actions.' Michelle then added, laughing, 'Then all can be forgiven and we instantly acquire our angel wings.'

By now we were all feeling more comfortable and the priest seemed to cotton on to Michelle's sense of humour. 'Okay . . . but it doesn't quite work like that?' Father Michael asked with curious sincerity.

'No,' Michelle said. 'Not quite. Our understanding of a life review is that it is a little less neat and quite a bit more complex than that. When we die we do not achieve instant sainthood or wisdom. Nor do we immediately let go of our personalities and experiences—otherwise communication through a medium would be impossible. Looking back, how was your father? Was he the same person you remember him to be?'

'Oh, absolutely!' Father Michael exclaimed. 'That's what upset me so much about all the other priests saying it was the devil in disguise. I knew my father, we were best mates! There is no way that man who met me over there was anyone *other* than my dad. I know it in my heart. I could feel how much he loved me . . . but there was more.

'When he was alive, my father used to sing a little ditty to me. Not a well-known song by any means but one he learned while working on the docks. The whole time I was with him, there were people singing that song in the background. The other thing was about me becoming a priest. One day, when I was just about to take my vows, my father pulled me aside and said, "Son, it's not too late to change your mind if you're not one hundred per cent sure. There are a lot of pretty girls out there—you'll be missing out on all of them!" It was a joke, of course, but one that let me know that he understood the sacrifice I was making for my faith. I knew he was proud of me then . . . and I knew he was proud of me when I saw him after the accident.

'Then I could feel myself being drawn back into my body by the same force that pulled me out of it. I didn't want to leave him. I was just so happy to see him again. Then, just as I was about to wake up, I heard him talking about all the pretty girls and I knew it was a reference to the conversation we had 30 years earlier when I was taking my vows. The ambulance officers said I came back to life laughing and crying. They assumed it was some form of euphoria triggered by chemicals in my brain, but I knew better.'

Father Michael came back to earth with a thud. His whole notion of what the afterlife would look like was shattered and rebuilt in the matter of a few minutes. 'It's funny though,' he continued, 'you would think it would have changed my ideas and beliefs but it only reinforced them. When I came back, I knew that my life as a priest was exactly the life I was meant to have lived. I have no regrets—not even about missing out on all the pretty girls! I guess I had a partial life review . . . but it's difficult to explain. It just sort of comes from the inside, as a knowing.'

Every spirit gets the opportunity to review their life when they die, but Father Michael had been given something even better: a glimpse at where he was at—and where he was going—while he was still alive.

Father Michael admitted to us that at various times during

his priesthood, he had lost his way. His midlife review had given him an insight into his soul's itinerary. He had an opportunity to test his faith and he knew he had made the right choice in becoming a priest, but now felt safe in expanding his horizons as well.

'When Dad told me to take in all the beauty of God's work, he was telling me to see the good in all religions and all faiths,' Father Michael explained. 'That is obviously what he became aware of in the afterlife. Because when he was here, he wouldn't have a bar of any other religion. Dad was Irish Catholic all the way.'

One of our favourite sayings has always been 'Spirits are people too.' It is an acknowledgement that although a soul no longer inhabits a physical body, it doesn't lose its capacity to think, feel or reach out to those it loves. 'Seeing Dad showed me that when my time comes, I will have the loving support of my family to help me with the process,' Father Michael added. 'That is very comforting.'

So what does the life review process actually involve?

As with most things, a slow and steady progress will ultimately yield the best results. Each spirit is free to face life issues or put them on the backburner and deal with one thing at a time. When you have spent a lifetime on the earth plane developing your personality, likes and dislikes and points of view, you can hardly be expected to let go of all that instantly. You need to review your life in context.

In the spirit world, to gain perspective you must be in a calm and balanced state. This is why every soul receives healing and spiritual orientation soon after crossing over. That in itself may take a while depending on the circumstances. If, for example, your death was traumatic or you are feeling resentful about leaving the earth plane, then the first step would be for you to reach a point where you are ready to accept the healing you need to settle into the spirit world. You are certainly not going to make too much progress if you are angry or agitated. Each spirit will reach this stage when their soul is ready.

Being ready to honestly accept personal responsibility for our deeds is the key to when our life review begins. The process is carried out in stages over time because we must be open to look truthfully at the life we have just lived. There must be time for your spirit to process that life without the limitations of carrying a physical body and the constant struggle for survival. We need time to absorb the implications of our actions and to pare down to the basics of our soul.

We all have interactions and relationships both good and bad with other people while we are here. Each experience has its own lesson to be examined. And it may well be that we need to wait to be reunited with a certain person before we can resolve our issues with them. For example, you were part of a marriage which didn't work out and you reach the spirit world before your ex. Because your itineraries and your experiences are intertwined, you may have to wait until they too are in the spirit world and in the right frame of mind and ready to address any relevant issues.

A life review encompasses an examination of our lives not only from our own perspective but from the broader perspective of others. Our actions have consequences and the life review process helps us to understand those consequences as they relate to others as well.

Sometimes the results can be a relief. Imagine that someone falls hopelessly in love with you but you do not return their feelings. Throughout your life you feel terribly guilty for the pain you caused them and often wonder what happened to them. Then, during your life review, you discover that, as a direct result of their heartbreak, they spontaneously decided to travel overseas. There they met the true love of their life and, during their lifetime they actually remembered you fondly, sending a silent prayer of thanks that everything worked out for the best.

However, the life review process is not about being judged by others—it is about self-appraisal and the soul growth that comes from sharing earthly experience with members of our spiritual family. These family members have undergone their own life review and know that it can be quite confronting. Their compassion and love for us smooths the way. Undoubtedly there will be some surprises too, because of the wonderful way in which our universe unfolds.

Your life review will encompass an examination of your spiritual itinerary. Here, you will be able to gain an insight into what your intention for this life was and how well you fulfilled it. Then, when the time is right, you will be able to decide what your next step is for continuing your soul journey.

'These are pretty big concepts,' Father Michael said, referring to our discussion of life reviews and what he experienced. 'They have given me food for thought.'

He also told us that, during his afterlife experience, he was shown a random event that occurred in his early twenties which he had barely remembered:

'I was shown a day long ago when a rather harassed-looking young woman and I both ran for the same taxi, arriving at the taxi at the same time. I was wearing my seminary clothes and felt obliged to make a good impression so I begrudgingly said, "Go ahead, you take it." All the while, I was privately thinking, "Go on, lady, I'll just stand here in the rain for another twenty minutes trying to get another one." I find it difficult to believe what an impatient young man I was back then.

'Well, although that woman was a stranger and had no way of ever letting me know it, my half-hearted act of chivalry allowed her to make it to her sister's bedside and say goodbye just minutes before she died. My father told me that in that stranger's mind, on that insignificant day in my life, she thought of me as an angel. Apparently even now she regularly prays for me. I felt bad for my surliness but uplifted too. It's strange.'

In the spirit world we are able to see connections between our lives and others more clearly than we can here on earth. Given that most of us are our own worst critics, the presence of loving members of our spiritual families during our life review prevents us from judging ourselves more harshly than necessary. On earth, it would be a great advantage to remember the main principles of the life review: the idea is to learn from our lives, not be punished for them.

'Seems to me that the life review process is partly about unlearning what we thought we knew,' Father Michael said with clarity in his voice. 'I'm a lucky one. I now know that I chose the right path in my life by becoming a priest. But you know what has really inspired me? It's knowing that everyone gets another chance. In the depths of my soul, I just knew that even if I had messed up, there would always be another chance to make it right.'

23
Dream connections

While some people have nights filled with wild and surreal dreamscapes, there are just as many who claim to have never had a dream in their life. Whether we are able to recall them or not, scientific studies have shown that we all dream every night. Physiologically speaking, the purpose of dreaming is to release day-to-day pressure from the mind, much in the way that a pressure release valve might work on an overinflated hot air balloon. By releasing all the hubbub, dreaming stops us becoming mentally overloaded. It enables our mind to slow down and rest. But for some people, the world they access through their dreams is a doorway to higher planes of consciousness: the planes of spirit and creativity. Many a great idea or new innovation is born of dreaming.

Setting aside the practical and physical benefits of dreaming, we have experienced and heard so many accounts of dreams being more than just a pressure release valve that the subject bears closer scrutiny. Are dreams simply our imagination or wishful thinking? Are our dreams just a way for the mind to let off steam, or, as mystics throughout the ages attest, are they actually more profound than that? Most importantly from our perspective as mediums, where does the spirit world fit in . . . if at all?

The answer is probably a combination of all of the above. The earliest records of dreams come from Mesopotamia and date back to 3100 BC. These days the occurrence and length of dreams can be scientifically monitored and measured, but because they are a deeply personal and emotional experience they cannot be explained by science alone. We can hook a person up to a machine that monitors which synapses in the brain are fired up during their dreaming, but the machine can't tell us what they are dreaming about or, more importantly, why certain dreams come at particular times in their lives. It is for precisely this reason that science and spirituality have been at loggerheads over dreams throughout the course of history.

We have both experienced so many strange, delightful and curious dream phenomena throughout our lives that we no longer subscribe solely to the scientific point of view. We fully acknowledge that dreams have a recuperative function for the mind but we know that, in addition to mental clearing, dreams also offer pathways to higher learning.

Many years ago, well before Michelle had explored her mediumship, her ex-husband's grandmother, Veronica, passed away. Ronnie, as she preferred to be called, was a lovely woman—vibrant, full of life and always with a twinkle in her eye. About two months after her funeral, Michelle had a dream about her.

Dressed in the same clothes that she wore to Ronnie's funeral, Michelle was sitting on a bus on the way to the memorial service just as she had been on the actual day the funeral was held. The bus stopped and Ronnie boarded, walked up the aisle, and sat next to Michelle. Everything about Ronnie was exactly as Michelle remembered her. She looked great, her hair and makeup perfect as usual.

Forthright as always, Michelle said, 'What are you doing here? I'm on my way to your funeral!'

'Yes, love, I know,' was Ronnie's calm, smiling reply. 'I just came to ask you to tell everyone that I'm alright. Could you do that for me?'

'Of course I will,' replied Michelle, still a bit shocked by the encounter.

When she woke up the dream remained with her in absolutely vivid detail. This was unlike any other dream. It felt *real*. It felt like it wasn't a dream at all but an event that had actually happened. Naturally, it also presented a dilemma— did she now actually do as she promised and tell Ronnie's family? Communicating with deceased relatives was not part of their normal routine or belief system. Undoubtedly they would think she was crazy.

This type of dream where a deceased loved one appears is called a visitation. Looking back, it is not so strange that this beautiful lady would choose Michelle rather than one of her own family to visit. In the afterlife, she probably had some inkling that Michelle would be working as a medium in the future. Had Ronnie chosen to visit her own daughter or one of her grandchildren so soon after her death, they would likely have dismissed the experience as nothing more than a reaction to their grief or the emotional strain they felt from settling her estate.

Michelle's experience is not unique. We have heard thousands of stories from people who have dreamed of a deceased loved one in such vivid detail that it stands out from their run-of-the-mill dreams. Visitation dreams make you feel like the person is right there with you. They are far more emotionally moving than normal dreams and usually make logical sense. Spirits who connect through dreams are often trying to reassure their loved ones that they are still very much alive and well, even though they are no longer physically present.

There are, of course, times when loved ones who have crossed over may appear in regular dreams where the subconscious mind is just filtering excess mental and emotional issues. These are not nearly as vivid and do not feel so profound. They don't pull on our heartstrings in the same way that visitation dreams do. They can contain nonsensical and surreal aspects where details are blurred and confused. Most people would be familiar with such filtering dreams. The kind where you might be in a house you *know* is not yours but in the dream it is your house. These types of dreams are important for our psychological health but they are very different from visitation dreams. They just sift through day-to-day events and issues, allowing us to let go of some of the mental energy we don't need. That is why they are often hard to recall—they are a way of letting go.

Many people also experience recurring dreams. Recurring dreams are important and we should pay attention to them. Some people have a recurring dream that first began in childhood and continues throughout their adult life. Others may experience recurring dreams during times of change, upheaval or trauma. These dreams, though they may seem cryptic, contain a subtext of guidance from our souls or our friends in the spirit world. They may act as a timely warning about an upcoming situation; they may provide the solution to a problem; or they may be a dreaming version of deja vu, letting us know we are on track with our spiritual itineraries. Our subconscious and spiritual influences are very clever— repeating the same dream ensures it is retained in our minds and memories.

Dreams can also be prophetic—warning people of danger or showing them opportunities they may have otherwise missed. Prophetic dreams usually leave us with a feeling that something is about to occur in the near future. This may be a personal situation such as dreaming of a long lost friend, only to find that the friend contacts you a few days later. Or, it may be of a more universal nature, such as dreaming of an earthquake. Unfortunately, more often than not, the meaning of a prophetic dream only becomes clear after the event occurs.

Information contained in prophetic dreams comes from the astral plane. When we dream our spirits can leave our physical bodies and, attached by the silver cord, enter the spirit realms. The astral plane is, among other things, an information superhighway like the internet. You can access things but they don't always have relevance to you. That's why so many of our regular dreams are rambling dialogues that make little or no sense. During sleep, we are simply in the flow of what some psychologists call the 'collective subconscious' or the 'universal mind'. This is the combined mind of everyone and everything in the universe; some may call it the mind of God. That is why some of what we hear, feel and see while dreaming doesn't relate to us. It is out there . . . but it is other people's business that we happen to notice as we are passing through.

While there are many people who don't believe that a collective subconscious exists, we have many great personal experiences that it does. On numerous occasions, we have shared the same dream. One time, we both dreamed that we were driving in a car that almost overran a corner because we were going too fast to see a bend in the road ahead. It was a message to slow down and carefully consider what we needed to do next.

It would be far too easy to dismiss our prophetic dreams as a by-product of our mediumship; a psychic phenomenon that is only available to the so-called 'gifted'. But prophetic dreams are the universe's way of giving us a heads-up into what is about to transpire and they can happen to anyone.

Upon occasion we have been asked by people who dreamed of a loved one's death before it happened if there was anything they could do to prevent it from occurring. The answer is no. The time of our death is written in our spiritual itinerary and is beyond our individual control. Dreaming of an impending death may be just the spirit world's way of gently preparing you for what is to come.

It should be noted, however, that not every death dream is actually about someone physically dying. There are spiritual deaths too. Many years ago, Ezio dreamed that a favourite uncle was about to die. Naturally he was shaken. Twenty-five years later that uncle is still alive. So why the dream? Looking back, Ezio's uncle was about to retire from work . . . and have a massive stroke that would leave him severely incapacitated. His death in Ezio's dream was not a literal death but rather a major change and upheaval. In short, the death of life as he knew it. Death dreams may be about change of circumstance—one situation dying and another being born. It is important not to take them literally or else you will live your life fearing something that may never happen.

When we are asleep our conscious minds are out of the way. We are not focused on our next task or our day-to-day lives. We are not distracted by our physical senses processing images and sounds, so we have some mental downtime. Just as it is much easier to get a person's attention if they are not driving, watching television, working or engaged in some other activity, it is much easier for our loved ones in the spirit world to have mind-to-mind communication with us when we are asleep and our minds are not full of other things. As in the case of Ronnie coming to visit Michelle, those in the spirit world will often take the opportunity during this lull in mental activity to make contact with their loved ones. This is especially true in the first few months after a person dies.

As time passes, it becomes more difficult for those in spirit to get through because they have moved deeper into the spirit realms. As we progress in the afterlife, our energy vibration becomes lighter and it is more difficult to push through the veil and into the physical world—even through dreams.

A good medium trains for years through meditation and ongoing practice to be able to receive information from the spirit world while they are awake. Brainwave activity during a full and proper mediumistic connection is similar to what we experience during the REM (rapid eye movement), or dreaming, stage of sleep. This has been borne out by scientific testing of mediums while they are conducting a reading. The implications of these findings with regard to consciousness and life beyond death remain in dispute within the scientific world. The debate is immaterial to us. Whether mediumship can be empirically proven is not the point. There is an old shamanic saying which states that effectiveness is the measure of truth. Put simply, this means that if something works, then it is real. This is *our* yardstick.

To engage fully with those in the world unseen, there is an orderly process of preparation and opening up to the spirit world. We have trained ourselves to raise our psychic and spiritual vibration to get our own minds out of the way and be open and receptive. We are not constantly in contact with spirits—even though we are constantly aware of their presence. This is often disappointing to people we meet outside of our working life who expect us to be on call to bring through their relatives at any given moment—whether at the beach or at a dinner party! But just as a plumber doesn't bring his tool kit along to a social gathering, we don't bring along all the spirits either.

It takes energy, effort and discipline to work properly as

a medium and not everyone has the dedication, aptitude or inclination to develop their abilities. Nevertheless, everybody sleeps and dreams so this is a wonderful way for those in the spirit world to get through directly to their loved ones who are not trained mediums. Visitation dreams are nature's way of ensuring we connect with our spirit family, people who have helped shape our lives and unfold our destiny. It takes effort for them to lower their own spiritual vibration and meet us halfway along the astral planes so we should treat visitation dreams as precious gifts and value them highly. Even if you do not consciously remember your dreams, don't worry—rest assured they do occur and your spirit receives what it needs. Your mind may forget but your soul remembers.

Visitation dreams are not the only type of dream that have that uncanny quality of realness to them, however. Dreams where we are actually astral travelling, as described in Chapter 14, can be every bit as real and vivid as visitation dreams. In children, astral travel dreams often take the form of flying. Many children describe hovering above their beds, flying out of the house and around the neighbourhood, witnessing events below from a bird's-eye view. Some have even spoken of learning how to manoeuvre around corners and bends, floating along hallways and playfully bumping into walls and doors. These dreams are not frightening because the dreamer is always in control of the direction they take. Certainly we both clearly remember having such dreams as children and that they were a wonderful uplifting experience. Maybe one day we will have them again. We have shared many dreams already—it's fun to imagine that we might share a flying dream too!

Perhaps these dreams are a metaphor for learning how to navigate life and all its challenges. But more likely these childhood dreams are the memory of the soul being free of the constraints of the physical body and going out to explore the world without fear, just as the spirit of the baby in its mother's womb is free to come and go. They are the last remnants of our memories of life before life, blending the feeling of spiritual freedom with the visual reality of the physical world we now inhabit.

Children are closer to the spirit world where they originated, which is why flying or floating is not so foreign to them and these dreams occur more frequently. As we get older and become more entrenched in the physical world, we become more anchored to the earth. Consequently, although adults do experience vivid astral travel dreams, it is much more unusual for them to actually 'fly' during their dreams. Maybe, like Ronnie, they simply catch the bus.

24
Travel tips for life

'I'm not afraid to die, Nanna,' Rebecca told her grand-mother, Monica, as she lay in her hospital bed. 'Don't be sad. I think I'm ready to go now.'

Rebecca was nine years old when she was first diagnosed with childhood leukaemia and within a year had exhausted all avenues of treatment available to her. Chemotherapy was no longer working—her body had stopped fighting the disease that would soon end her life.

'Hush, Becky,' her grandmother told her, holding back a flood of tears. 'There is plenty of fight left in you yet, my beautiful girl. There are still so many things for you to do. Besides, you come from a long line of fighters so don't start saying that you're ready to leave me.'

'Okay,' the young girl said tiredly, closing her eyes as she spoke. 'I'll fight if that's what you want me to do.'

In her heart, Monica knew that all the fight had gone out of her beautiful grandchild. She could see it in her eyes. Rebecca's bright blue eyes had once been filled with life and playful mischief; now they were sunken, dull and grey. Monica felt guilty asking her to fight on so that she wouldn't have to endure the agony of losing her. She reached for Rebecca's hand and held it gently, knowing that this brave child had given everything she had in her fight against this dreaded disease. It was time to let her go. 'Alright dear,' she said. 'I know . . . if you are really tired and need to let go then just do it, my love. It will be like going to sleep. I won't try and stop you. But Becky . . . please . . . just make Nanna one last promise?'

The young girl opened her eyes, startled that her grandmother had anything to ask of her. 'Yes, Nanna, what do you want me to do?'

Monica smiled wanly at the dying child. 'When you get to heaven, tell your mummy and daddy that I love them, will you?'

Monica told us the story about losing her daughter and son-in-law in a fatal car accident while they drove north on their summer holidays six years earlier. Rebecca had been only four years old at the time and had escaped without injury. 'She came out of the accident with barely a scratch. My daughter and her husband were killed instantly. I remember thinking at the time that if God wanted my daughter and son-in-law for some particular reason, then I guess I had no right to argue with him. Maybe it was their time. I consoled myself with the idea that he left me with Becky to look after and raise as my own—to help take away some of my pain. She was my strength as I mourned my daughter. Then Becky got sick,' Monica said, shaking her head in disbelief. 'Leukaemia, of all things. Can you believe that? Such a terrible disease.'

It's ironic how many stories we hear of people surviving one tragedy, only to be taken out of this world by another. There was the case a few years ago of a European tourist narrowly escaping injury in the Bali bombings only to be mauled to death by a crocodile when he arrived in Australia a week later. As uncanny as such stories appear, they understandably give rise to the idea that when it's time to go, it's time to go.

Monica came to see us for a private consultation a few years after Rebecca had crossed over. She was unsure what to expect and came along with an open, if mildly sceptical, mind. 'I'm not sure I believe in the afterlife,' she warned us. 'Well, I do—sort of—but I have never had a reading before and don't know what to expect. I came because I could no longer stand the thought that Becky had just vanished into thin air. Becky was such a beautiful child. She has to be worth so much more than that. Before she died, I told her that she was going on a holiday, to meet up with her parents again who had gone ahead and were waiting for her. I didn't know if that was true or not—I just didn't want her to be frightened. I hope it was true.'

We always feel the pressure to make the spiritual connections that people are hoping for. You might call it professional pride, but it's more than that. Getting in contact with the spirit world can sometimes be a tricky business—especially when the client divulges so much information beforehand. Normally, we would have stopped Monica from telling us so much, but from her nervous demeanour it was obvious that she needed to talk. The problem with a client telling us too much before a strong link has been established between worlds is that a great deal of what they say could have been used by the spirit as evidence. Being given too much information before a session limits some of what we can pass on as the client is aware we already know it.

Those in the spirit world will do everything they can to help us deliver a great reading but, in the end, it always boils down to one thing—the client's need. Real need always makes for a better reading. By telling us that she wasn't sure about the afterlife, Monica wasn't intentionally laying down a challenge to our mediumship, she was being open and honest. We could tell that, though sceptical, she was secretly hoping we would prove her wrong. More than likely, she just didn't want to walk away disappointed.

If there is a genuine need for the healing and comfort that a good reading can deliver, it always makes the connection to spirit so much stronger. Over the years, people have come along to see us for all manner of reasons—some more noble than others. We once had a rather rude woman enter our reading room clutching a handful of photographs and demanding that we use our abilities to spy on the people in the pictures. Naturally, we refused. Mediums are not spiritual guns for hire. Our abilities are not meant for spying, personal gain at another's expense, or, as in the case of that rude client, revenge. They are meant for healing broken hearts and wounded souls. Healing, bringing comfort—that is the reason we feel so much pressure to make a good connection every time.

We watched as Monica fidgeted uncomfortably in her seat, clutching the handle of her handbag so tightly that her knuckles turned white. We motioned for her to put the bag on the floor beside her, an offer she declined.

'Perhaps she thinks you will steal it,' our spirit helper Marcus joked. 'Tell her not to worry, we have a very good connection to her daughter.'

'Just try and relax,' Ezio told her. 'Take a deep breath and go with the flow. We will connect into the spirit world anyway we can. Sometimes, they make it easy to determine who is communicating and sometimes it's a bit like a game of charades. One spirit opens the door for another so even if the person you want to get in touch with doesn't come through first, please accept them graciously because they are part of the process. Spirits link to one another like a daisy chain in order to bring each other close enough so the medium can perceive them.' It is our usual spiel, delivered before every reading. It seemed to help Monica relax. She took a few deep breaths, exhaled loudly, then loosened her grip on her handbag so that the colour began to return to her hands. We were ready to go.

'There is a lady here by the name of Julie,' Ezio told her immediately when the session had begun.

'Oh my God,' Monica gasped, forgetting herself as her handbag fell to the floor. 'Julie is my daughter!'

'She is showing us The Big Banana—Coffs Harbour in northern New South Wales. That is where the accident happened?'

'No . . . well, yes . . . sort of,' Monica stumbled over her reply. 'It was about fifteen minutes outside Coffs Harbour. They were on their way there. That was where they were planning to holiday.'

Coffs Harbour is a famous tourist destination on the mid north coast of New South Wales. Aside from its warm climate and stunning beaches, its distinguishing feature is 'The Big Banana', an oversized fibreglass banana that tourists can walk through to learn about the local banana industry. Silently we thanked Marcus for his expertise in connecting us to Monica's daughter with such clarity. Monica's daughter Julie and her husband Robert had been travelling for five hours and had almost reached Coffs Harbour when a driver travelling in the opposite direction strayed onto the wrong side of the road and smashed head-on into their car. The information was so precise, Monica had to accept that the spirit of her daughter was really communicating with us.

Julie went on to show us that she was present at the moment when Becky crossed over by describing the scene in detail. Ezio tried to relay it as faithfully as possible, to reassure Monica we were truly in touch with her daughter. 'I can see Becky laying in her hospital bed, you are seated at her side. A dark-haired nurse walks in and touches your shoulder. It is a sign of empathy and compassion. At the moment that your grandchild takes her last breath, her mother and father are both there to escort her through the veil between worlds. You are telling her something . . . that it's okay for her to go . . . No, that's not it . . . you are . . . you are singing to her!'

Monica started laughing and crying at once, unable to

stop. Three years of pent-up emotion poured out of her like a waterfall.

At the end of the session, we assured her that telling Becky she was going on holidays with her parents had helped her cross over more smoothly than she might have done. 'It was exactly the right thing to say,' Ezio told her. 'Especially considering how her parents had died. Becky would probably have died sooner, but she didn't want to leave you. She loved you very much. In her heart, your granddaughter died believing that she was going to pick up where they left off and enjoy a nice sunny vacation with her mum and dad. What could be better than that?'

Monica leaned back in her chair and exhaled deeply. 'Thank you. I don't know what else to say. I am shocked and delighted . . . Becky is with her mother . . . I feel a weight has been lifted off my shoulders.'

When Monica told her granddaughter that she would soon be heading off to enjoy a wonderful afterlife holiday with her parents, she had no way of knowing if it were true or not. It was a bittersweet theory, and now, hopefully, one that we had proved correct. But the notion of leaving this planet and going on vacation was more than just a beautiful metaphor created to soothe a frightened child. It is a spiritual truth presented in a way a little girl could understand. Becky's mother and father had not abandoned their child, they had gone ahead of her, preparing the way, making sure that she would see familiar faces and have loving arms to embrace her upon her arrival in the next world.

Our life on earth is an adventure. For Becky, that adventure was now over and had shifted to another plane of consciousness: the next phase of life. Granted, for some people the adventure is more pleasant than it is for others. That is the way of destiny. If you look back over your life, a pattern emerges. You can see the big moments clearly. Meeting your wife or husband, finally landing that big job or contract, the birth or death of your child. When counted against the backdrop of a lifetime that lasts around 75 years such moments are few and far between. Yet they shape everything else around them.

These big events are our destiny; they are our spiritual itinerary talking to us. Everything else is just padding, things we do to fill the time and lead us to the next phase of learning and spiritual growth. These pivotal moments provide the experience that our soul carries from lifetime to lifetime. So, looking at life, knowing that we count the important things on the fingers of one hand, what can we take away from the experience? As intrepid travellers who have traversed the landscapes of time and place, religion and culture, what travel tips will we leave behind that might make the journey of those who follow a little easier than our own?

Throughout this book, within each and every story, and from each and every spirit, we have received a travel tip. If we reflect upon what they have learned, we can apply their advice right now to help us live better lives. Each has their own perspective, but as we look at some of the main ones we see the appearance of a common theme.

We know from wise women such as Shondra that everything on earth has its time and will eventually fade away. We also know that everything in the spirit world is eternal and will not fade. The cycle of life is unbroken, death an illusion of the physical world. We can take comfort from this knowledge, for we will all most certainly see our loved ones again in this world or the next. All that is required of us is patience. Shondra said it best when she told us, 'Spirit is where we come from . . . spirit is our home.'

We have ridden a wave of raw and painful emotion with T.J.'s family as they lost, mourned and continue to endure the stages of grief at the tragic passing of their brother and son. T.J. is a revelation. His account of what it's like to live and die is priceless. Like an explorer he has ventured into the greatest unknown—death—and returned to share with us a firsthand account of what it is like to die. T.J. may have only been sixteen when he died but his insight and ability to communicate from the spirit world is a precious gift to us all.

T.J. taught us the importance of standing up for your 'crew' and, more significantly, that we are all connected so *everyone* is your crew. From his experience we have learned that hatred towards those who have wronged us is futile. It is written in the big plan for our lives. At some stage, everyone will be a victim or a perpetrator. His perspective and attitude from the spirit world shows that no matter the circumstance, love and forgiveness is always the answer. It is then that our soul begins to heal and we can grow. As T.J. so eloquently explained to us when talking about the young man who ended his life, 'You can't really blame him for doing what he was born to do, can you?'

Possibly not, T.J. But down here we need time to reach that level of understanding. By standing alongside his family as they fight for justice, T.J. has realised and accepted this also. So, for those of us still here, it is about striking a balance. We can't ignore wrongdoing, but we must address it and then find a way to move forward so that we begin to heal.

Such notions are naturally difficult to accept. How do we forgive and love those who have hurt us deeply? How do we take the knowledge that we are all players in each other's drama and turn this into enlightenment? It is not easy. Perhaps it is the struggle to love and forgive that is our true purpose on earth. Nevertheless, life and love exist on both sides of the veil. Therefore, there is really no such thing as an 'afterlife' per se. The very word, afterlife, conjures the idea that a new life begins when this one is finished. Life is never finished. It's all about stages. When our time here is done we move into a different time zone, a different phase of the *exact same* life we always owned. Even if we find this concept complex, our souls know it is true.

Red Eagle gave us the key to striking the balance. He surprised us with his tale of being a twelve-year-old merchant sailor who, having experienced a difficult lifetime, emerged with a rare insight that is the essence of soul growth. When asked what he had learned from being so horribly mistreated, he stated, 'I learned that unless I forgave those who hurt me, I would always be their victim.' It is worth remembering that the love and forgiveness we need to find benefits ourselves, our own souls, most of all.

And what of Joel, the Guru of Surfing, or Shelley, queen of the kids? Two human beings who came to earth and touched the hearts of so many with their grace and compassion. While others shed tears for them, their hearts breaking a little more each day as the physical condition of these brave spiritual warriors deteriorated, their own souls shone brightly into heaven where their friends and family were gathering to meet them. They both knew they were going home. Joel looked at his mother as she cursed the dreaded disease multiple sclerosis, smiled lovingly and said, 'Mum, it's a gift.' Through his own suffering he discovered what was truly important: 'We are here to love.' A simple truth that is easily lost in the business of life.

Shelley inspires us with her consideration for others. She knows the value of not losing touch with your loved ones. Caring for children in the spirit world, she helps bring them to the families they left behind. Shelley knows that parents never let go of their children, emotionally or spiritually. She works tirelessly in the spirit world to bring kids into contact with their earthly families so that those on both sides of the veil might heal. Shelley has given us great insight into the power and beauty of selflessness—a virtue often forgotten here on earth. When asked why she didn't tell a friend that she was dying of cancer, Shelley shrugged and said, 'She was so excited about her holiday that I didn't want to ruin it for her.'

Without question, the message that those who have lived, died and come back to tell the tale most frequently share is that love never dies. Like our souls, love is indestructible. We are starting to suspect that this is because our souls are the physical manifestation of love itself. Ah, how it all comes back. That is what Red Eagle meant when he said that our souls are the part of us that is God.

Our souls exist beyond this life, this excursion into the physical world. We are eternal. Our time here with all its trials and tribulations helps us understand the emotions and attributes that make love grow, making the soul grow too. Compassion, forgiveness, even letting go of the ones we most care for when it is time, are all noble acts.

We also learned a valuable life lesson from Monica. By whispering to Becky that it was alright to give up the fight and let go, Monica displayed a far greater act of love than she realised. She had smoothed the progress of Becky's soul, even though it broke her own heart. There is no greater act of love than surrendering what you need for the good of another.

As Monica stood to leave the room after her session, Ezio heard the angelic voice of a young girl singing a familiar, happy tune. It was Becky!

'What is she singing?' Monica asked.

The melody grew louder, gradually becoming clearer and clearer. It was a song he had heard many times before. A little self-consciously, he sang her the tune 'Summer Holiday', made famous by Cliff Richard.

Monica smiled. 'Thank you. It means so much more than you know. That was the song I sang to her when she died . . . the one you mentioned that my daughter Julie heard me singing. I don't know if I will ever be whole again. My heart is so broken. But at least I know they finally got to have that holiday together. Maybe one day I will join them.'

Life. The journey continues . . .

About the authors

Ezio and Michelle De Angelis are Australia's best-loved husband and wife psychic medium team. Working both together and independently, they travel the country conducting public and private sessions of survival evidence mediumship. Their work has been featured on television and radio and they regularly contribute to a variety of mainstream magazines and publications.

For over fifteen years, their work in reuniting people with their loved ones in the spirit world has brought great comfort and joy. They are also highly renowned and sought-after as teachers and mentors by those wishing to develop their own mediumship abilities and spiritual gifts. Together they own and operate the acclaimed teaching centre, The Gathering, located in Sydney, Australia.

Michelle and Ezio were both made Honorary Lifetime Members of the Australian Psychics Association for their tireless work and support of mediumship.

Ezio is the 2012 Australian Psychic of the Year, an award conferred by his peers.

www.eziodeangelis.com.au

T.J.

15/11/1993–30/10/2010

Joel
8/02/1982–24/08/2008

To see Joel on YouTube, search 'Our Guru Of Surfing'
http://www.youtube.com/watch?v=0vSUrrCZM2c

Shelley
31/12/73–21/06/2005